# BUSES
## ANNUAL 1985

*Front cover:* **The Volvo Citybus chassis reintroduced the concept of underfloor-engined double-deckers to Britain. The prototype, with Marshall body, is seen in service with Strathclyde PTE in Renfield Street, Glasgow, in 1983.** *Gavin Booth*

**£4.95**

A memory of the famous interchange at Cheltenham, with coaches loading for the 1500hrs mass departure. This August 1983 view shows coaches of AEC, Bristol and Leyland manufacture, from the fleets of various NBC companies and the independent Yelloway. More pictures start on page 97. *T.W. Moore*

# BUSES
## ANNUAL 1985

*Edited by Gavin Booth*

LONDON

IAN ALLAN LTD

First published 1984

ISBN 0 7110 1404 3





Published by Ian Allan Ltd, Shepperton, Surrey; and printed by Ian Allan Printing Ltd at their works at Coombelands in Runnymede, England.

# Contents

# Fetters Rent in Twain

**ALAN MILLAR on the post-1980 scene**

The bus industry establishment had a fairly cosy half-century from 1931, when road service licensing was introduced and newcomers were first required to prove that their new services would fulfil a need that neither existing bus services nor parallel railways could satisfy. That cosy existence was shattered in May 1979 with the election of a Conservative Government.

Margaret Thatcher's first Transport Minister, an ambitious ex-journalist and former Opposition transport spokesman, was Norman Fowler, who had already expressed his objections to controls being placed on the development of the bus and coach industry. He wasted little time in transforming his ideas into legislation, and the 1980 Transport Act received the Royal Assent towards the end of June that year, ready for a series of fundamental changes to bus licensing over the next few months.

Fowler's most radical change was to abolish all road service licensing for excursions and tours and express services of over 30 miles. No longer need an applicant face months of opposition in the traffic courts from established operators and railwaymen before ending up, as often as not, with strict conditions on the number and size of coaches to be used on the route. Instead, provided he notified the Traffic Commissioners 21 days in advance, he could operate. If the service fails, that is his risk.

For stage carriage services, Fowler's instinct probably was to adopt the same approach and sweep away all capacity controls, but he was more cautious. The 1980 Act turned the tables on objectors at a traffic court hearing, and instead of leaving the new operator to prove that his service was necessary, it was the objector's duty to prove that the new service was against the public interest. The Act did not specify what was meant by the public interest. There also were powers to designate trial areas in which all road service licensing would be abolished, in order to establish whether a free-for-all could apply across the country.

The Traffic Commissioners' weary hours adjudicating over applications to vary fares (a pathetic euphemism for 'increase' in these inflationary times) ended with the Act. The Government reasoned that the scope for competition removed the need for this late remnant of price control, and the Commissioners were glad to rid themselves of this thankless task at the earliest opportunity. Conductor licensing also was abolished, but outside London the conductor had

*Left:* **Typical of the exotic machinery used by some of the private coach fleets competing on Scottish express routes, an integral Van Hool Astron used by Newton's of Dingwall in Perth on the Edinburgh-Inverness service in 1983.** *Ian Train*

*Right:* **Remember British Coachways? In the red, white and blue BC livery, a Grey-Green Leyland Leopard/Duple at the rather makeshift Kings Cross 'coach station'.** *Ian Train*

*Right:* **An invitation to travel? The entrance at Kings Cross in 1981.** *Kevin Lane*

also more or less been abolished.

That was only one side of the equation. To ensure that lives were not put at risk by the more competitive environment, an operator licensing system, similar to that which had worked wonders in improving lorry standards in the 1970s, was introduced in place of the individual vehicle licensing system used hitherto. Vehicle testing standards were also tightened up, with annual vehicle tests replacing the long established one-to-seven year certificates of fitness.

It will be several years before the real benefits of the O-licensing system and annual testing become apparent, but the Traffic Commissioners are convinced that standards will rise. National Welsh and Central SMT have already been given public warnings about their maintenance standards, other companies have faced hearings, and some small enterprises have lost their licences for failing to meet the minimum standard.

The effects of Norman Fowler's deregulation, by contrast, have been more immediate, especially in the coach sector. While road service licensing was not abolished until October 6, 1980, at the end of the summer peak, many operators took advantage of the new freedom and took up the Transport Minister's challenge to be the 'Laker of the coach lines'. Independent airline chief Sir Freddie Laker, whose Skytrain service led to transatlantic air fares being cut from 1977, was still a national hero three years later, although the collapse of his airline early in 1982 ended the public adulation.

That Laker label probably stuck fastest to British Coachways, an ambitious attempt to establish almost overnight what the National Bus Company had taken decades to develop. It brought together six of the largest independent operators to run express services from London to Glasgow, Birmingham, Liverpool, Manchester, Bristol, Exeter, Plymouth, Cardiff, Swansea, Middlesbrough and Newcastle. Grey-Green provided coaches from London, and managed a terminal at Kings Cross which, while reasonably centrally located, fell short of the far from ideal standard of NBC's ageing and cramped Victoria Coach Station. The provincial partners were Wallace Arnold, serving Yorkshire and Devon, Shearings-Salopia, serving the North-West of England, Ellerman-Bee Line, serving the North-East, Park's of Hamilton, serving Scotland, and Morris of Swansea, serving South Wales. They were joined soon after by Barton Transport and York Brothers of Northampton, providing London-East Midlands journeys, Excelsior from Bournemouth, and by Warner-Fairfax, from London to Bristol.

If British Coachways drew inspiration from Laker, it pinched its advertising slogan from British Airways. In place of 'Fly the Flag', Coachways urged travellers to 'Ride the Flag' and the red, white and blue livery of its member companies' coaches bore an uncanny resemblance to the airline's familiar identity. It pitched its fares below those being offered by NBC's National Express, and courted travel agents to direct business its way. It aimed to operate a better overall class of coach than National, with reclining seats fitted to many of the Leyland, Volvo and MAN coaches that dominated its fleet at the beginning.

It had a good start, with Norman Fowler cracking open a bottle of champagne before the first Grey-Green Leopard set off for Scotland on October 6, but was running out of steam after four months. Fares were increased and names given to the principal services for the 1981 summer timetable, but the consortium was disintegrating. York and Warner-Fairfax pulled out first, disappointed by poor business, Grey-Green was out by July, and any credibility ended when Wallace Arnold opted to run its services alone from the autumn. It abandoned its West Country services in January 1982. The surviving partners were left to run the services as their own or give up, and the only ghost of this brave venture is Grey-Green and its fellow Cowie Group subsidaries' use of the Coachways livery style for their coaches.

The Shropshire-based Whittle Group was another to take immediate advantage of the new freedom, and bought five Duple-bodied Leyland Leopards – its first heavyweights for many years – for two services linking Shropshire and West Midlands towns with central London. These continued to operate, but from spring 1981 were co-ordinated with National Express routes and terminated at Victoria, rather than Kings Cross. Others were to do the same.

Two independents did better on the routes from Scotland to London, where traffic on the long established Scottish Bus Group services had begun to flag. Cotter's of Glasgow, a highly professional tour operator, introduced its Coachline service just before Christmas 1980, linking Edinburgh and Glasgow to the capital with Van Hool Alizée-bodied Volvo B10Ms equipped with videos for on-board feature films, taped music, galleys and staffed by stewardesses. The fare was pitched just above the SBG and Park's rates. A much newer company, Perth-based Stagecoach, which had taken early advantage of the new Act to run a Dundee-London service as GT Coaches, using an ex-West Yorkshire PTE Volvo B58, started an Aberdeen-London route early in 1981, again with stewardess and on-board catering. It has expanded to use double-deck Neoplan and Van Hool coaches, and in 1983 started the first direct Inverness-London overnight service. Stagecoach has also exploited the relaxation of stage carriage rules to run internal Scottish limited stop routes on stage licences, generally using similar high specification coaches.

It would be wrong to imagine that SBG has lain down in the face of such successful competition. Interest in its London services has revived, and it has expanded internal express services to meet the new demands. It has also begun to dabble with stewardess service, and is the first British customer for Metro-Cammell Weymann's Metroliner double-decker, having got in ahead of National Bus with an order for six for delivery in time for the 1984 season. The prototype entered trial service from Glasgow to London in April 1983.

At the opposite end of the spectrum, coach operators have been able to win a share of commuter traffic, especially in London where more journeys exceed 30 miles and where even a small percentage of the total commuter market represents a healthy income for the operator. It can also mean a great saving for the customer over the sometimes astronomical annual rail season tickets.

Most of the services are single coach operations from the 'stockbroker belt', providing a guaranteed seat for office workers not prepared to pay for the same from British Rail. A notable exception is the group of services which has mushroomed between the Medway towns and North Kent and London, where a large population is served by an indifferent Southern Region rail service. One Medway independent, Olsen's, captured a sizeable share of this business very quickly, eventually using up to 27 coaches a day, many of them Ford R-Series models which had just ceased to be required for contract work at the Isle of Grain power station site. This was another Laker-style operation, and its own success was short-lived as financial troubles cost it its O-licence in January 1982. However, the services thrive, mostly now in the hands of Grey-Green, which has discovered a form of deregulation with which it is much happier.

The limited success achieved by independents in England contrasts sharply with a huge revival in the fortunes of National Express which, from losing 14 per cent of its traffic in the nine months before

*Left:* **A Cotters Volvo B10M/Van Hool Alizee on the up-market Coachline service from Scotland to London.** *Kevin Lane*

*Below:* **Several of the companies exercising their new-found freedom used double-deck coaches. A Park's of Hamilton Van Hool Astromega in Glasgow's independent coach station.** *Ian Train*

*Foot of page:* **Several of these Neoplan Skyliner double-deck coaches have been bought by Stagecoach, the Perth independent.** *John Burnett*

deregulation, had built up its carryings by 50 per cent in 1981 and by 75 per cent by 1982, when rail strikes helped swell its coach stations.

It carried out a major market analysis survey during 1980, retimed many services, launched new fares deals, and began a television advertising campaign using Beeper, a cartoon frog with voice-over by disc jockey Kenny Everett. Unlike most of the independents, National had reasonably civilised coach stations (notably in London), could market its services nationally, and had booking agents in most towns and cities. Travel agents were also more inclined to book passengers with National than British Coachways. Its local subsidiaries were encouraged to launch their own express routes, and as with the independents, these did best in London. Deregulation has brought new business for London Country's Green Line, for the Oxford-London City Link network which rapidly disposed of competition from the independent Heyfordian Coaches, for Alder Valley's Londonlink services along the M4 to Thames Valley towns, and for Maidstone and District's Invictaway routes which give good competition for the independents on the Medway towns routes.

Where National has been weakest is in the quality of its services. A few hours spent queueing and confused in the mayhem that is a busy day at Victoria can deter all but the most cost conscious of travellers, and independents prepared to offer services comparable with those of the Scottish operators have given National a run for its money.

Trathens, the Plymouth international operator, started running a superior service to London in November 1980, using coaches which would run empty to London anyway to meet commitments there, and a small Exeter company, Glennline, introduced a similar service from its base. It was later taken over by Trathens. Wallace Arnold went up-market when it pulled out of British Coachways, providing a hostess service from Yorkshire and games tables on the Devon routes from which it eventually was squeezed out by competition from Trathens and National.

The solution for National was simple. It reached a joint marketing deal with Trathens from November 1981, acting as booking agent for its own basic services and Trathens' luxury routes which were marketed as National Express Rapide. Trathens started using Neoplan double-deckers on the Plymouth Rapide routes, and hired some of its own vehicles to National for use on Rapide services to Exeter and Swansea, pending delivery of Duple-bodied Dennis Falcon V machines for National's own fleet. Rapide services were extended to Manchester and Yorkshire in mid-1982, the Yorkshire services incorporating Wallace Arnold's operations, and the network has grown further since then.

It too has its rivals. Isleworth, Middlesex-based Len Wright Travel uses a Van Hool Astromega on a full-luxury London-Manchester-Blackburn route, and London-based Blueline uses high-floor Setras on a highly popular Newcastle-London service

*Left:* **In London's Baker Street on one of the growing National Express network of Rapide routes, up-market services with video and hostesses, a Midland Red Leyland Tiger with high-floor Plaxton Paramount 3500 bodywork in October 1983.** *Kevin Lane*

*Right:* **The Scottish Bus Group's network of express coach services was marketed under the Scottish Citylink name from October 1983. In blue and yellow Citylink livery, an Eastern Scottish Leyland Tiger with Plaxton Paramount 3200 body on the X14 Edinburgh-Glasgow express service.** *John Burnett*

established some months before Rapide reached Tyneside.

National also co-operated with the private sector in February 1982, when it started a joint marketing deal with Magic Bus, an agency providing cheap international coach travel to young persons. Magic Bus was given access to the hallowed sanctum of Victoria, but disgraced itself the following Christmas by folding up abruptly and leaving passengers stranded across Europe. National formed Supabus, its own successor business, in time for the 1983 summer.

None of this, of course, was quite what the Conservative architects of the 1980 Transport Act had in mind, and Norman Fowler's successor, David Howell, included powers in his 1982 Transport Act for any NBC subsidiary to be privatised in order to increase private sector involvement in coaching. He wanted NBC's property to be developed in partnership with private developers, something NBC was happy to do if it could expand its cramped and ageing terminals, and for the coaching activities to be sold off. NBC was far from happy about this, especially as coaching is integrated into the total NBC business, and by 1983 the Government appeared to be moving on to wholesale privatisation of NBC, which would keep the business intact.

The other public sector, the local authorities, have made some forays into deregulated coaching. Reading and Southend Borough Councils marked October 6, 1980 by running a joint service linking the two towns with London and Heathrow Airport. They were split into separate routes, Reading to London, and Southend to Heathrow, in May 1982, but they offer sufficient business for both operators to run special double-deckers on them. Reading runs MCW Metrobus and Leyland Titan coaches, Southend more opulent three-axle Van Hool Astromegas.

Burnley and Pendle started its City Flyer service from Colne to London in May 1982, and a year later was joined by Leicester and Maidstone Boroughs when the route was extended into a Dover-Blackpool marathon. Lothian Region, which began expanding its Edinburgh city tours programme to British and European destinations in 1981, started express coach services to St Andrews and Aviemore in 1982, reached Inverness the following year and started a joint Edinburgh-Blackpool express with Lancaster City Council.

The growth of coach operation in Britain, together with a tenfold increase in coach shuttle traffic between Britain and Europe over the same period, has generated demand for more luxuriously appointed and more durable coaches. Heavy duty and integral construction models, many imported pending the development of new British models, have taken the place of the motorised skateboards that operators were prepared to buy when business was less brisk and the customers were less discerning. It is doubtful whether domestic work alone would justify the six-figure sums which some of the new breed of coaches command, but the

*Left:* **The adventurous but ultimately unfortunate CK Coaches challenged Cardiff City Transport's service network in 1981/82, using ex-London Transport Daimler Fleetlines like the former DMS 1552, seen at Cardiff bus station.** *Ian Train*

*Right:* **Yeowarts of Whitehaven created much interest when services were started in competition with the nationalised Cumberland company. In all-over yellow livery, an ex-Fishwick Leyland Leopard PSU4A/2R with 44-seat Fowler body, in Whitehaven.** *Ian Train*

combination of lucrative shuttle work, some deregulated express services, and deregulated excursions business has helped enliven a hitherto stagnant industry.

As yet, the same cannot be said about stage work, which has continued to decline, despite the scope for some competition. There have been some notable cases of new blood being allowed in, but also some setbacks and outright failures. Three examples spring to mind.

A Cardiff independent, CK Coaches, was granted authority to run two city services from April 1981, two months after the Government abolished Cardiff City Transport's monopoly powers. CK offered lower fares, conductors to help passengers on and off its buses, and had the advantage of being able to buy fairly cheap ex-London Transport Daimler Fleetlines. Cardiff responded by retiming services and offering fares reductions, and there were various allegations of the two operators' drivers trying to run one another off the road. But it was a short-lived venture, for CK ran out of money the following winter and the service was abandoned at the end of March 1982.

Yeowart's Coaches' endeavours to run town services in Whitehaven brought the might of National Bus around its neck before it finally gave up in 1983. This was a small coach company which bought secondhand Leyland Leopards from Fishwick's of Leyland and applied to run a circular town service. The Northern Traffic Commissioners turned down the application, after Cumberland Motor Services threatened to withdraw rural services which were subsidised from the profits of its Whitehaven routes, and it was only after Yeowart's appealed, and Norman Fowler disregarded his own inspector's advice, that a licence was granted in 1981. Cumberland responded by beefing up its Whitehaven service and withdrew six rural services in a blaze of self-generated publicity. Cumbria County Council challenged the Government's decision in the courts, and Yeowart's was forced off the road in January 1983 when the Court of Appeal ruled against the Government. Yeowart's sought authority for new routes soon after, but these were turned down by the Traffic Commissioners and the company withdrew a subsequent appeal and sold its buses.

The fortunes of Tyneside-based Low Fell Coaches have been happier. It spotted the potential for a direct service from South Gateshead to central Newcastle early in 1982, after Tyne & Wear PTE cut most cross-river routes to feed into its Metro station at Gateshead. Low Fell won authority that summer for an experimental route, survived an attempt by Tyne & Wear and NBC to have the decision over-

ruled by the Government, and was granted a full five-year licence the following year.

As this was being written in August 1983, there were only three trial areas in operation, as few county councils were very keen to participate in the scheme. The first, in North Norfolk, covers an area with so few buses that the removal of road service licensing has made no difference. A second in Hereford and Worcester started in 1981, but the county has taken over the Traffic Commissioners' role there by getting operators to tender for a basic network of routes. It has led to some exchanges of service between operators. The third scheme, in Mid and East Devon, started in August 1982.

Future developments could see much greater stage service deregulation, as the Conservatives' 1983 election manifesto hinted at giving private operators a greater role, possibly in a complete free-for-all. But their first priority is London, where the freedoms of 1980 have been curbed by other legislation.

Any operator wanting to run in London is bound by the 1969 Transport (London) Act to reach a London bus agreement with London Transport, which is bound to consider whether the overall needs of Greater London will be met by such a move. The result has been that few competitive services have been granted, and the few which have were the result of expensive appeals to the Government. Commuter coaches from parts of North Kent within the Greater London Council's area were started by Bexleyheath Transport in 1983, after David Howell overturned LT's earlier refusal.

LT's most dramatic challenge came around the same time when Amos, the popular name for Associated Minibus Operators, sought authority for a service of 400 16-seater minibuses in high frequency competition with LT on four cross-London routes. LT's independent inspector found little difficulty in rejecting the application after Amos presented a weak case at a lengthy public hearing, dismissing it as a folly, but the company was determined to appeal.

A White Paper published in July 1983 proposed giving private operators an opportunity of going behind London Regional Transport's (the name for a renationalised LT) back and letting them apply to the Traffic Commissioners instead. Even if Amos is never heard of again, another ambitious independent could stand a better chance, and uproot the bus industry in the same way as coaching has been already.

Coaching, too, could grow more if British Rail closes significant stretches of secondary lines and makes road travel more attractive. Certainly, times will not be cosy for a long time.

**Photographs taken by G.H.F. ATKINS at London's Victoria Coach Station between 1934 and 1958 illustrate the evolution of coach design.**

*Right:* The distinctive radiator and cab of Midland Red's own-make SOS LRR type of 1933 vintage, with Short 30-seat coach body, seen in 1934.

*Below:* An East Kent Tilling Stevens B49C2, one of 23 new in 1931 with Brush 32-seat bodies, seen in 1934. It lasted until 1948, and was one of the last of its type to be withdrawn.

# Memories of Victoria

*Right:* **Loading up in 1937 involved the driver of this Western SMT Leyland Tiger TS7 with 32-seat Leyland body, new in 1935, climbing on to the roof to fill the rack. The coach was on the London-Glasgow service.**

*Below:* **Another 1935 delivery was this handsome Eastern Counties Bristol JJW with Eastern Counties 32-seat coach body. One of ten, it is seen at Victoria in 1937.**

*Below:* **In September 1949 a new Aldershot & District Dennis Lancet 3 with curvaceous Strachans 32-seat coach body, one of 15 used on express services to London.**

*Foot of page:* **In 1947 Southdown received 25 of these Leyland Tiger PS1/1 with Eastern Coach Works 31-seat coach bodies. The first of the batch is seen in September 1950.**

*Below:* **Newer Southdown Leylands, Royal Tiger PSU1/15 with centre-entrance Leyland 41-seat bodies, seen here in July 1952.**

*Foot of page:* **Against a varied selection of billboards, a new South Midland Bristol LS6G with 37-seat ECW body at Victoria in July 1952.**

*Below:* **A Maidstone & District Bristol L6A with 35-seat ECW bus body, a combination more normally associated with Tilling fleets. Compare the body with the more elaborate Southdown version on page 16.**

*Foot of page:* **Two United Bristol LS/ECW coaches rest in Eccleston Place, near Victoria, after the long trip from Newcastle in July 1954.**

*Below:* **Unusual bodywork by Lydney Coachworks was fitted to 19 Leyland Royal Tiger PSU1/13 for the Red & White fleet in 1951. One is seen in September 1954.**

*Foot of page:* **Double-deckers with coach seats have long been a feature of the London-Reading service. This 1951 Bristol K6B with ECW 53-seat body is seen in September 1958.**

# A Transport Career in Retrospect

## R.C. LUDGATE on working in Ulster

My first introduction to the various intricacies of public transport came in November 1945, when I joined the former Belfast and County Down Railway Company (affectionately known as the 'County Down') at Queen's Quay Station, Belfast. I commenced work in the stationmaster's office, followed by a short period in the goods office and later in the main passenger booking office. This also included a very interesting period in the railway control office.

To digress for a moment to put the reader in the picture, it should be mentioned that in 1946 the then Northern Ireland Government issued a White Paper on public transport in Northern Ireland as a result of which, some two years later, on October 1, 1948, the Ulster Transport Authority (UTA) was formed to amalgamate the railways (which at that time were in the financial doldrums) with the Northern Ireland Road Transport Board undertaking. On that date the NIRTB and the B & CD Railway undertakings were merged, leading eventually to the complete abandonment of the County Down system by April 1950. This was followed on April 1, 1949, by the takeover of the LMS Railway, the 'Northern Counties Committee' which had managed the railway on behalf of the British Transport Commission in London, up until that time, when it was duly dissolved.

The Great Northern Railway (Ireland) had approximately two-thirds of its entire network in Northern Ireland and the remainder in the Republic of Ireland. In 1953, the two governments (both North and South) passed an Act simultaneously to form the Great Northern Railway Board (note that 'Ireland' in the title has been replaced by the word 'Board'); the Board consisted of some ten members (five from each country), and this resulted in the dissolution of the owning company, namely the GNR(I) undertaking. This was a prelude to further Acts being passed in 1958, which eventually divided all the assets of the newly-formed GNR(B) between the UTA and CIE (Coras Iompair Eireann). Thus the UTA had by October 1, 1958, gained control of the entire Northern Ireland railway network. In breaking up the UTA monopoly in the mid-1960s, the government of the day established the Northern Ireland Transport Holding Company – responsible for all transport activities through its subsidiary companies – Ulsterbus Ltd (road passenger services – except Belfast Corporation Transport); Northern Ireland Railways (railways) and Northern Ireland Carriers (road freight services). Ulsterbus therefore

*Left:* **UTA Leyland Leopard PSU3/3 no. 481 was one of four 'Wolfhound' express coaches introduced in 1965. The livery was grey and white with a maroon band.** *R.C. Ludgate*

*Right:* **This unusual UTA bus was a Bedford VAL14 with UTA 56-seat bodywork, seen when new in 1964.** *R.C. Ludgate*

*Right:* **Former Stockholm D924, a right-hand drive Scania Vabis-Capitol that was used by UTA for a short period in 1967. It is shown outside Duncrue Street works.** *R.C. Ludgate*

assumed responsibility for all former UTA road passenger services on and from April 17, 1967.

Moving on a few years now, I recall an interesting happening as far as bus enthusiasts were concerned, when in 1966 a limited amount of competition was allowed, whereby sections of unremunerative UTA routes in the Craigavon (County Armagh) and North Antrim areas were disposed of to two new private operators – Sureline Coaches Ltd of Lurgan, County Armagh and Coastal Bus Services Ltd, Portrush, County Antrim respectively. Whilst Sureline remains the largest independent operator in Northern Ireland, Coastal was unfortunately forced into closure in April 1974, as a result of adverse economic conditions, with its services and small fleet of buses passing to Ulsterbus.

Some years later another event to recall was the merger between Belfast Corporation Transport and Ulsterbus; this had been scheduled to take place on April 1, 1973, but this did not happen for a number of reasons. Instead the powers of the Northern Ireland Transport Holding Company were extended by the creation of Citybus Ltd, which under a management board common to that of Ulsterbus, assumed responsibility for all the former Belfast Corporation Transport services.

This would now be an opportunity to recall the various changes over the years of the various company liveries, starting with that of the NIRTB undertaking, which was light green with dark green waistband and medium green mudwings. As far as UTA was concerned, it simply reversed the dark and light colours in both fleets, and roofs were painted cream. In 1951, two new Leyland Royal Tiger luxury coaches 8930/1 (MZ 7965/6) were painted in a light blue-green livery with dark green flashes on the wheel arches, cream roof and extensive chrome trim on waistband and along the bottom of the body panels. Further variations in this colour scheme were later used on coaches and dual-purpose vehicles. During 1959, a light unrelieved blue-green and cream livery was introduced for double-deckers (mainly the Leyland PD3/4s) and this scheme was continued on all subsequent new vehicles, with the older buses remaining in the green livery.

A further new livery of Elizabethan Blue/Hyacinth Blue was introduced in 1961 for touring coaches. In the last year of UTA operations (1966/67) several batches of second-hand buses were hastily acquired and some were put into service in their original owners' colours, including 15 ex-

*Above:* **The 1,000th bus built by UTA, Leyland Titan PD2/10c no. M636 in 1958.** *R.C. Ludgate*

*Above right:* **The first bus in public service in the new Ulsterbus livery, an ex-Edinburgh Leyland Tiger Cub PSUC1/3 with Weymann bodywork in 1966.** *R. Ludgate*

Western SMT Leyland Leopard L1s; some 45 ex-Ribble buses which comprised 38 Leyland Royal Tigers with Leyland bodies and 7 MCW-bodied Olympics and finally 48 Weymann-bodied Tiger Cubs which came from Edinburgh Corporation.

1965 saw the introduction of the UTA's first 36ft long coaches for express workings – these were Leyland Leopard PSU 3/3s, with an unusual design of body, built by the operator at the Duncrue Street workshops. Finished in a grey/white colour scheme with dark maroon flash, they carried the outline of an Irish Wolfhound dog on both sides. Fleet numbers were 481-4 (2481-4 OZ), which were followed in 1966 by two 30ft long similar type coaches (485/6-2485/6 OZ). These six coaches operated with the fleet name 'Wolfhound' and were the last vehicles ever built by UTA.

A refreshing change was brought about when Ulsterbus introduced a livery of Riviera Blue and Ivory, with variations on coaches and dual-purpose vehicles. At the outset it was one of the ex-Edinburgh Tiger Cubs, which had the honour of carrying the fleetname of the new company, albeit experimentally at first. This was 9034 (SWS 34), which carried the fleetname 'Ulsterbus' in ivory, lined out in black using 10 in high italic capitals with squared serifs, the whole name being spaced to an approximate width of eight feet, centred on the blue background. Later it was the turn of sister vehicle 9013 (SWS 13) to emerge into the limelight, as the first bus to appear in public service with the new style fleetname carried on the side panels.

This arrangement lasted for a short time, until the fleetname was reduced in size, enabling it to be carried on the waistband, along with the company logo. This livery is still in use today, the only exceptions being that during the early 1980s, luxury touring coaches were painted in Riviera Blue and Monaco White. A few of the ex-Ribble Royal Tigers carried their red livery until 1968, whilst

there were also a number of former UTA colour schemes existing until early 1969.

Some significant dates and important events from a wide area of interest in my recollections. One of the most memorable was in June 1958, when the 1,000th bus built by UTA rolled off the production line in the Duncrue Street works; this was a Leyland PD2/10c double-decker, fleet number M636 (WZ 636), the chassis of which was originally a Leyland PS2 (fleet No 8809) with B34F body built in 1949. The body was removed and the chassis rebuilt by UTA, using running units from PS2s, before being fitted with a new H32/28R UTA/MCW body. This was just one of 158 similar type buses built between 1956/58. The demise of this type took place on Saturday December 30, 1972 (a miserable wet and windy day!), by which time only four such buses remained on passenger duties (the driving school had several which lasted for a while longer before being replaced by PD3/4s). The four in traffic on that day were 641/2 (WZ 641/2) and 707/27 (UZ 707/7727). However, the honour of being the last half-cab-rear-entrance double-decker operating in public service fell to 642, when it worked the Belfast (Oxford Street)/Ballybeen service (route No 8) until the last run of that duty, which was the 1830 to Belfast (the other three had finished their various turns of duty earlier that day). This then marked the end of an era in public transport in the province.

Another vehicle of interest was built in 1964 – a solitary Bedford VAL14 with UTA B56F body, which entered service on April 1. Carrying fleet No T118 (2318 GZ), the rather ungainly-looking bus had a very high waistline, rather small windows and unfortunately met an untimely end, when hi-jacked by terrorists in Strabane on November 30, 1973 and completely destroyed.

There were many demonstrators over the years, particularly during the UTA regime, but perhaps the most unusual one appeared in 1967. In that year Sweden changed over to driving on the right, thus rendering a large fleet of Scania Vabis-Capitol buses superfluous in Stockholm. One of these, a 1956 two-door single-decker, found its way to Belfast, arriving on February 10 at the Duncrue Street works. This was *Stockholms Sparvägar* no D924 and it travelled to Belfast from the Swedish capital by sea to the port of Immingham, thence overland to Stranraer, finally reaching Northern Ireland by the ferry to Larne Harbour. It was given temporary registration 920 TZ before entering public service on March 1 on the Londonderry city service route

**September 1962, and an interesting selection of UTA buses at the Great Victoria Street bus station, now much changed.**

between Shantallow and Clooney. Some minor modifications had to be made before the PSV authorities in Northern Ireland would grant permission for the bus to be operated, even for a short experimental period. In fact, it lasted only 18 days before the bus was withdrawn from service due to a mechanical fault. Shortly afterwards it returned to the mainland and nothing further came of the experiment. The author believes that the UTA was the only undertaking in the British Isles to test one of these buses.

One-man operation was first introduced by the UTA during 1962 and was extended gradually over the years – but it was not until November 28, 1976, that it was fully implemented by Ulsterbus on all its services throughout the province. As far as the Belfast Corporation Transport undertaking was concerned OMO was first introduced on September 1, 1969, on a number of selected routes, and completely finalised on November 13, 1975.

It is interesting to reflect on some of the changes to bus stations in Northern Ireland, particularly in Belfast, over the years. Smithfield bus station in Winetavern Street, in Belfast's city centre was the terminus for the road passenger services of the former LMS (NCC) Railway and passed to the NIRTB in 1935.

Then in turn it was taken over by UTA in October, 1949 and again by Ulsterbus in April, 1967. From 1969 onwards it suffered a number of bomb attacks by terrorists before being totally wrecked by bombs on June 11, 1977. The ruins were finally demolished and the site cleared to become a car park! All the services were then transferred to the bus station at Oxford Street in East Belfast, which had been opened on July 15, 1960. This was built on the site of the old Belfast Central Railway terminus and on part of the original Maysfields goods marshalling yard of the former GNR(I) system. Sited immediately opposite Smithfield bus station, was North Street bus station, built in 1928 and originally the headquarters of the old Belfast Omnibus Company. This also in turn passed to the NIRTB, the UTA and finally to Ulsterbus in 1967. It had been closed to bus operation during 1966, but was used for a time as a bus park by Ulsterbus before eventually being sold in August, 1967; subsequently it became a vehicle park for Post Office vans etc. To complete this brief resumé of bus stations, it should be noted that when the Belfast terminus of the former Great Northern Railway in Great Victoria Street was finally abandoned on April 24, 1976, the new Central Station that replaced it was built on the site of the former Haymarket trolleybus depot of Belfast Corporation Transport. The old railway terminus lay derelict for a number of years, before being finally demolished, but one small section of the original station canopy, which was over platforms 4/5, still remains and can be seen to this day incorporated in the present Ulsterbus Glengall Street depot.

There is one little anecdote which should not go unrecorded. It was in a quiet suburb of South Belfast in the early 1950s, when I was officially photographing a former UTA Leyland PS1 single-decker, which had been converted to a mobile library for the Belfast Public Libraries. I was approached by an elderly lady, who had been observing me at work with my MPP 5in×4in plate camera, complete with the black head-cloth! She wanted to enquire about borrowing the books which were yet to be supplied and I had to help her up the steps of the vehicle before she would accept my story that it was empty – she was very disappointed on seeing the rows of shelves without their books!

In conclusion the many years spent working in public transport have been varied and interesting in more ways than one, leaving me with many pleasant and nostalgic memories. Needless to say, my keen interest in the world of buses is still being maintained to this day.

Alexander ex-Ribble Leyland TD4/English Electric in Glasgow. *Allen T. Smith*

**Caledonian challenges for JOHN E. DUNABIN**

# Sorties into Scotland

Being excursions – or, depending on one's point of view, incursions – from England.

Perhaps the precursor of all these, in the strict sense a non-event, whetted my appetite, but if that hadn't done so something else would have provided the stimulus.

The occasion was a short camping holiday on the south eastern edge of the Lake District, and with no motorised transport of our own available choice fell on the bus/coach. Direct travel was too inconvenient – working this out from Lancashire United and Ribble timetables with their fascinating maps aroused an interest I have never lost – so we went via Liverpool.

Publicity matter for the service, newly inaugurated the previous year, mentioned three operators, Ribble, already a familiar name, and not just one from Scotland but two, Scottish *Motor Traction* and Scottish *General Transport*, creating immediate fascination. I sampled the first-named of these two on the return journey, memory remaining of tyres rasping on the underside of the wheel arch as we cornered rather fast, particularly when the driver was very late in deciding to take a right fork, but the scarlet 'Transport' vehicle was the one that got away. All else seemed to be of Leyland origin; perhaps this was a TS Express coach flashing past.

After that, with little opportunity for actual visits, Scotland, developing as a romantic concept in my mind, fascinating if rather frightening, had to be savoured through other eyes, firstly those of R. L. Stevenson with the dramatic opening scene in *Kidnapped* and the later hunted journeys of Allan Breck. I went on to read everything of his I could find, even *St Ives*, only half-written by RLS himself and finished by an Englishman, who added flights by balloon to more mundane travelling, by 'claret coloured chaise' or even 'following a covered cart'. Then came John Buchan, who could make anywhere from the Border to the industrial belt and again beyond exciting in past and present (but he never let Richard Hannay, user as I remember it of every other form of transport, come down to riding on buses), and even, one must admit, *The People's Friend*, with its succession of stories about nice girls from the country, whose romances were deferred, making good in their own Glasgow teashops – they got there by tram of course. It was a world full of light and colour.

But the most fascinating book of all, fat and modestly priced, though not, one hopes, to be regarded entirely as fiction, was the *Scottish*

*Omnibus Timetable*. Who for example was it wanted to journey every Saturday for 8 minutes from Bo'ness to Top of Flints, and never to return? Mystery and excitement were there. To have acquired such a massive tome by post, even in those days, would have been expensive, but it could always be purchased without having to cross the border. One threepenny bit (three old pence) handed over the counter of the SMT office in Trafalgar Square was enough.

The next actual expedition, when we, a fellow explorer and myself, really did reach Scotland, was markedly different in almost every way. Nine years had gone by, taking with it much of the storybook view of the terrain, and while bus enthusiasm had captured me – incompatible with too much dignity or studied indifference to the mode of travel – things around were subdued and perhaps a little austere. This was 1940, and the trip north was hurriedly planned after two or three postponements.

An overnight rail journey from Manchester – overnight, that is, if one accepts four hours spent in front of the fire in the porters' room on Hellifield station as part of the trip – brought us to Dumfries well into Sunday morning.

Pausing only to book accommodation at one of the best hotels in the town – 8/6d (42½ pence) in those days bought luxury, deep, comfortable mattresses in a beautifully clean and spacious room with a full 'English' breakfast to follow – we headed straight for Whitesands. Here, even though it was a Sunday, buses in a fair variety of colours, greater than that of makes certainly, were ranged out backing on to the river like a concours d'elegance. Spoiled for choice, it seemed best to make for the seaside, so Clark of Glencaple, Gibson of Moffat with his crimson/maroon coloured Leyland – come back to them in another 20 years – plus a range of Caledonian vehicles were ignored, and we headed for New Abbey and Rockcliffe on Mr Carruther's bus, another Leyland as I remember it.

This was Sunday, but the bus filled up tight before leaving, and I did wonder whether as 'foreigners' we might be asked to get off. No, and we got down to the coast, to watch a solitary aircraft engaged in bombing practice on an inshore sandbank, following this by enjoying one of the biggest teas I have ever eaten, priced at a shilling.

Returning by Caledonian from Dalbeattie left only a vague impression, no more, of a Leyland TD1, but the next day, before continuing by the afternoon train to Newton Stewart, a trip to Moniaive appeared to fill the time in nicely and provided more to remember. One can say that it was wetter at the outer terminal outside than inside the bus – we sampled Moniaive air for two or three minutes – but not much; the roof of the Caledonian Lancet was porous.

The following day taught me something about the limitations of public transport in parts of Scotland. We set out to walk to Loch Trool, just a gentle 10 mile stroll, and then, attracted by the lovely countryside, went on beyond. Returning, a good lunch at 'The House of the Hill' put heart into us, and we rejoined the main road from Ayr. The Western service we knew was infrequent, three times daily I think at that time, but those last nine miles, hoping the bus would overtake us but only knowing its time to within an hour, seemed rather long. We were perhaps on our thirty-third mile when it passed us in Newton Stewart's main street. For a more vivid picture of where we walked, *The Five Red Herrings* by Dorothy Sayers cannot be bettered, although she doesn't allow her characters to use buses either.

There wasn't much scope for travelling in Scotland after this for quite a while, and nearly another decade had elapsed before I crossed the Border again. This, though, was the real thing, Bridge of Don, Sauchiehall Street, Paisley independents, and a glorious trip down the west coast of Kintyre, all in one year.

Paisley was – still is, except when the sun blazes down – a grim-looking town, although made better if one sees some of the older parts of Glasgow first, as I did. Glasgow, though, had a river, and Youngs' buses, double-decker Albions in a sand-coloured livery, added to the attraction of the view from the south bank. Paisley, as I said, looked rather grim, with its high brown sandstone tenement blocks presenting an almost unbroken front to the street, but there was the brightness of the buses to offset this. In the main street there was, in my brief stay, always a bus in sight, often a reddish maroon Western decker, more frequently a sand brown Albion of Youngs. McGills in deeper maroon colour and Smiths in a forgotten, obviously less striking livery appeared, often enough not to be overlooked, from points south. Graham's buses I never saw at all – they only became noticeable, very much so, when Youngs vanished, and chameleon-like they adopted the vanishing Young livery, but just round the corner were others, Cunningham in green and white, Paton in light blue and white; all were double-deckers.

That doesn't quite exhaust the list. Mr Ferguson's dark green Victor buses were still running to and from Renfrew Ferry I think – how else would I remember their livery? – and Garners certainly were around, but I shall never reach John o'Groats if I try to enumerate everything. From this point of view, ignorance of which of the 22 constituent members of A1 it was whose bus I boarded on a hurried sortie to the west coast is perhaps a good thing.

I was ostensibly travelling home, but it didn't take

Outside the Western SMT office in Dumfries in 1950, an ex-Caledonian Dennis Lancet with ECW 32-seat bus body, new in 1937. Although in Western ownership, it still carries Caledonian livery. *Allen T. Smith*

all that long to hop off the train at Kilmarnock, find the small cave-like A1 bus station, catch the bus – they ran to Ardrossan every five minutes – break at Irvine to look around, catch another, off again at Saltcoats to sample the Clyde Coast service (the two overlapped over this section and still do) for the short distance to Ardrossan, and then return by A1, the same livery but perhaps a third member of the association, to Kilmarnock.

Later in that year I enjoyed a summer holiday in Kintyre. For my companion I have no doubt the highlights were different, but for me they were all connected with transport, not forgetting the trio of musicians, an old Clyde steamer tradition, on the boat from Largs to Campbeltown. Dismissing the overnight journey by coach from Bolton to Glasgow, better than the return ten days later but not good, the first stage, without waiting for breakfast, was by Young's bus, double-decked and almost certainly Albion, all the way to Largs. This was a good start, a clean bus, and pleasant country once we left Paisley behind, with a promising view of the Clyde estuary as we descended into Largs after an hour and three quarter journey. It seemed a mystery where the traffic came from to justify five buses an hour on Saturdays and Sundays, but it obviously did.

Kintyre offered different pleasures. Apart from one return journey by MacBraynes, evening in, early morning out, passenger transport there was in the hands of two independents, McConnachies up and down the west coast, reaching north as far as Tarbert, with a shorter route, an early rail replacement, to Machrihanish, and West Coast. West Coast did serve the west coast as well, along with MacBraynes and McConnachies, reaching up to Lochgilphead, but they had the east coast of the peninsula to themselves. Staying at Carradale, where it had a dormy shed housing an apparently unused OWB, we saw more of its operations. The West Coast livery was the ubiquitous red and cream, but McConnachies used something much rarer, darkish grey/blue with a hint of green below the waist, pale grey/green above, and a high gloss finish.

A round trip by West Coast to Tarbert, then down the west coast, gave us an exhilarating and luxurious ride in a prewar Leyland coach of McConnachies, but the real highlight was the return from Carradale to Campbeltown for the Saturday morning boat. We have solved it all now by one-manning, but on this occasion one conductor, with co-operative weaving in and out by the drivers, collected fares from four packed buses. He left us at least four times on the 14 mile trip. Our bus was a 29-seat OB Bedford, or was it a Commer? Some of the others, however, were bigger. West Coast conductors worked hard on other days too. A morning trip from Campbeltown out to Carradale included newspaper deliveries, non-stop of course, straight out or up and over, while on the return there were numerous stops for milk collection.

After this, another journey to Scotland a month or so later might have been an anti-climax, but business took me to Aberdeen, and gave me a spare afternoon. Strachan's maroon-coloured Fodens departed for Ballater, Balmoral etc from a small garage just down the street from my hotel, but I left it too late, being captivated by Mealmarket Street and its surroundings. The first surprise was a pile of attractive booklet timetables on the counter in the Sutherland office, with a 'help yourself' (at 2d each) attitude. Then, across the street at two wooden kiosks/huts, timetables of Simpson's and Burnett's buses were freely available.

A few minutes of intensive study and a clear prospect emerged. Two quick return trips to Bridge of Don and a little beyond – a little beyond just in case there was some restriction on carrying short distance passengers – could take in four operators, including Mr Daniel of Whitecairns, who still looked independent although his services appeared in the Simpson timetable. It all went like clockwork, with buses running bang on time at or near the end of a 20 mile plus run, and the operation was completed in about half an hour. Sutherlands were running newish double-deckers, the rest rather nondescript single-deckers. The latter had closing doors of course, and so, to my surprise, had the red and yellow rear entrance Sutherland Leyland, probably a PD1. I believe the company was the first to enclose rear platforms in this way; on that day, as we felt the force of a near gale off the sea, it seemed a very good idea.

Of course, there were still many buses left unsampled between Aberdeen and the Border. It seemed a pity to let them all pass by, or rather to pass them by, so I managed, by the right choice of trains, to squeeze a little diversion into the return journey home. Coatbridge and Airdrie proved to be very ordinary places, nothing wrong with them, nothing in general to enthuse over, but Coatbridge in particular was full of bright blue single-deckers, a good mix of AEC and Leyland makes, running to various pleasant sounding – again pretty ordinary really – destinations such as Carnbroe, Old Monkland, and Glenmavis. Baxter's buses dominated the scene here.

After this Scotland was neglected for a few years, apart from a quick trip to see Edinburgh for the first time, Castle, Royal Mile, New Town, Waverley Station, and the trams. Excitement enough, even though there were no cable cars any more, but neither, so far as I was aware, were there any buses around other than those of Edinburgh Corporation and the SMT group. In other words, rather less than perfect. Then circumstances changed, and I found myself only 40 miles or so south of the Border in February with a couple of days to spare. Possibly an earlier February trip to Glasgow, which included the hurried sampling of Youngs, Cunninghams, A1, AA, Clyde Coast etc, had given me the wrong impression, but to go north in winter seemed a pleasant idea.

A train from the South stopped conveniently at Motherwell, with Hamilton, where the real 'bussing' was to start, a mere two miles away. It was dark, damp, and cold in Hamilton, but the Chieftain buses of Lauries, all noisy, all double-deckers, prewar Leylands or utility Guys, provided enough attraction as they pulled up and departed every few minutes. My destination was East Kilbride, then just starting to grow as a New Town. All I registered in the dark was a very wide, wet and icy road, which I had to cross to catch the Glasgow bus.

If one relied on timetables rather than on-the-spot observation, the buses of David Lawson of Kirkintilloch, taken under SMT's wing some years earlier, were rather elusive, and in Glasgow, a big city, one had to search carefully for them, their livery being little different from those of the more plentiful Central and Western vehicles. No fleetname was blazoned on their sides either. Once found, the bus was another rugged utility Guy Arab decker, which gave me one of the roughest rides ever, but this was not the fault of its springs. I had planned to reach Loch Lomond, but a few miles of bumping over frozen snow made me think again.

Kilsyth, with different attractions to offer, beckoned instead. It wasn't far away, the bus service (Alexander's) was frequent – I was beginning to understand that in much of Scotland buses were frequent or non-existent – and, most important, I believed that from there Mr Carmichael operated the oddly named Highland bus service to Coatbridge. With no idea of how often it ran, I was delighted to spot a dull crimson single-decker Albion waiting in a side street as we passed. Planned or not, not by me anyway, this was a real spot connection. The service was well patronised by intermediate passengers, frequent – I saw three or four vehicles on service coming the other way – and closely supervised by a roving inspector, known to me as a 'jumper', but perhaps the Scots have another word.

The next highlight was even more striking. There had been tantalising news in the technical press over the previous year and more of new independent stage services on the eastern edge of Glasgow, a little pocket perhaps overlooked by the mighty GCT and the equally mighty SMT, so after a quick dash to Salsburgh on Mrs Greenshield's bus – no point in missing a chance so easy to take – I headed west along the tram route, but dropped off short of Glasgow at Shettleston.

There, perhaps three miles away from the

Highland terminus at Coatbridge, visible from the main road, were several units of the Lowland fleet, busily engaged in their rightful business. A couple of ex-Ribble Leyland Cheetahs – this from memory as are all other references to vehicle makes and types – in an unexciting grey, black and white livery didn't impress, but there was also a brand new (that very day) double-decker Leyland, glistening in a pale olive colour reminiscent of the well known and longer lasting Fishwick livery. I would like to think I rode in or at least saw one of the prototype Atlanteans that day, but memory won't come sharply enough into focus after so long.

That day must have been an elastic one, or did I stay for another night in Glasgow? According to my very basic notes the enjoyment continued, with Paisley re-visited and journeys by Smiths to Nitshill, McGills, and Grahams. After that Scotland didn't see me for six years; I wasn't exactly resting, just busy elsewhere.

1960 doesn't appear in the record books as a particularly severe winter, but it has a special place in my catalogue of cold journeys. Heading north on a February day which seemed mild enough in the Mersey valley, I made for Leadhills, only fifty miles north west from Carlisle, but the highest village in Scotland. That on its own was not, of course, the attraction. Mr Wallace of Leadhills had for long run the only bus service there, and although he had now left the scene it still remained in independent hands. To start with I had to get to Sanquhar, humdrum Western all the way from Carlisle now Caledonian had gone, but no matter; better things were ahead. Sanquhar is an ideal place for catching shy retiring buses, one broad main street and only two ways out, north west and south east. My quarry was an OB – the ubiquitous OB in those days – and while there were enough passengers on the 3.55pm departure most of them were schoolchildren, and all had gone, well before we reached Leadhills. The timetable was scrupulously honest, with one journey terminating there and another starting in the same direction half an hour later. The driver got out to have his tea, but let me stay inside, a welcome gesture on a cold grey day. One elderly passenger joined me and then, perhaps a little after his official time, the driver re-appeared.

Action stations! The old man soon got off, sleet started to fall, and the driver decided he needed to go faster. I couldn't see through my side of the screen, but he obviously had personal radar. Pell mell down by Elvan Water, sharp left, filter without pausing into the A74, off to Crawford – situated on the 'bad' side – and on again, then a fast breakaway to the right at Abington. Perhaps he was hurrying away from this accident black spot! Another fork, left this time, to Roberton, moving even faster with the screen nearly obscured by slush. I reflected briefly that the total loss of life would probably be small, there only being two of us.

Alighting at a most unlikely and truly rural terminus, St John's Kirk – Mr Leith only reached Lanark on three days of the week – all was peaceful, calm and dry, if not bright. Darkness was gathering however, and the appearance very shortly of a Central bus bound for Glasgow via Lanark was welcome.

Bus enthusiasts on safari commonly waste little attention on such things as board and lodgings, deriving nourishment from diesel fumes and snatching sleep only when there is no bus in sight, but I was looking for a little winter warmth in Lanark. Shown to my unheated hotel room, I was surprised to see the large sash window fully open – no place for taking things easy, so I retreated downstairs. Here, all that offered for rest and relaxation was a small alcove just inside the front door, so going out to look at, possibly even to ride on buses seemed a reasonable alternative despite black ice all around.

They were in serious difficulties, along with other traffic, on the climb up from Glasgow via Kirkfieldbank, but who wanted to ride on yet another Central bus anyway? With cautious steps I made my way down the winding road to New Lanark, Robert Owen's famous model industrial settlement 400ft below the town, just to have the pleasure of riding up again in Mr McKnight's Bedford.

Next morning, having discovered that Hamilton Jackson's Regent did not run on that day to Strathaven – 'we call it Strayven' said the Central 'clippie', leaving out the middle syllable – I headed south again, but only as far as Beattock. Two operators, Gibson, running from Dumfries, and Elliott from Lockerbie – or was it Turnbull by this time, also sporting a blue band? – connected the station with the nearby small town of Moffat, but both seemed to concentrate on passengers going to and from the south, so to have time enough for lunch there hot-footing seemed desirable. I was in sight of Moffat, personal radiator steaming – the day was still cool but bright and sunny – when I heard the familiar Leyland throb, but 2d for perhaps 300 yards seemed worth it, and having made my return intentions known to the driver I enjoyed an excellent lunch in the Buccleuch Arms, while presumably he did likewise in another place. Then followed one of my best travel bargains ever, twenty-two miles to Dumfries for two shillings.

The attractions of the Southern Uplands remained, so although a year later Edinburgh was the ultimate goal, I found myself in Lanark again. Remembering the difficulties over Strathaven, I boggled about asking for a return to Lesmahagow, but somehow, with the co-operation of Mr

*Left:* **Delivered new to David Lawson, then an Alexander subsidiary, in 1944, a Guy Arab II with lowbridge 55-seat Roe bodywork. It is seen in 1951 at Glasgow's Dundas Street bus station.** *Allen T. Smith*

*Above:* **In the smart silver livery of the Ayrshire co-operative operator Clyde Coast, an ex-Glasgow Corporation Leyland Titan TD5 of 1937 vintage, with Cowieson 56-seat bodywork.** *Allen T. Smith*

Jackson's crew, I got there and back. Time was neither for nor against me, there being enough, but a February evening is no time for hanging about in unfamiliar places, so I only allowed myself about 15 minutes to wait in the deserted main street of Carnwath, where, pretty well in keeping with his timetable, Mr Wilson's OB appeared.

There are in round terms a dozen main roads radiating from Edinburgh in a 180 degree arc (ignoring the Forth Bridge), but in the broad swathe between the A71/A704/A706 to Lanark and the A702 Biggar, Crawford, and the south, partly filled by the Pentland Hills, there is only one, the A70. This, the only artery into the city left unserved by SMT or its associates, was and is the shortest route from Lanark, but offering little intermediate traffic. Mr Wilson, however, was doing his best with a limited service. There were only few of us when we left Carnwath, but for the last fifteen miles into Edinburgh passenger loading dropped to two. Luck was with me; this was the last ever Monday journey apart from July and August operation. The service vanished completely a year or two later, and Castle Terrace, its Edinburgh terminus, once busy with Caledonian buses, possibly with those of Andrew Harper earlier, became just an ordinary street.

The better known attractions of Edinburgh were still there of course, unchanged, and there was variety in buses not far away. No Coast Line sadly, but from the same area Mr Wiles of Port Seton had been much in the news with take-overs, service changes, etc, and seemed to merit a visit. The bus I caught was a Scottish-built one I noted, or I might have thought it was the spiteful English getting their own back for something that happened at Prestonpans in 1745; we drove past the battlefield in a juddering Nimbus, a bad ride, reminding me of childhood days and lifts in overloaded 1914-18 vintage lorries.

With John o'Groats still in mind though, I must hurry on. Scotland called again the following February but the excursion was a modest affair.

*Left:* **The Albion Nimbus was never the most refined of buses, but East Lothian independent Wiles of Port Seton found them useful for stage work. This Alexander-bodied MR9 came from Leyland Motors.** *Gavin Booth*

*Below:* **The sole independent working into Edinburgh in the 1960s was Wilson's of Carnwath. Here at the Castle Terrace terminus in 1965 was an Albion Victor FT39 with Duple bodywork.** *Gavin Booth*

First to Dumfries, a circular trip past the grim-looking Caerlaverock Castle by Mr Clark's veteran Leyland, then on to Lockerbie, regretfully eyeing Mr Rae's smart blue normal control bus – was this a small Guy, or perhaps a well kept elderly Dennis? – heading for Boreland, and on to Moffat for the night by Blue Band. Next day, in glorious winter sunshine as we climbed out of the town, came a superb run by SMT to Selkirk and Edinburgh, then back to Beattock and home.

I have mentioned the Nimbus. Another product of about the same time which didn't seem quite right to me – after all, Bedfords catered for this end of the size range better – was the Leyland Comet. A trip later that year, really planned around abbeys and castles, included a circular trip from Kelso through the Cheviot foothills, organised, for all who wanted to travel by stage carriage, by Mr Atkinson of Morebattle. His Comet has, I am sure, long since fallen to earth, and the service too, no longer running nearly empty through empty country, but an enjoyable memory remains.

More sorties were to follow at irregular intervals – a five year gap now followed – seeking out the vanishing independents but reassuring myself that some of them were still thriving by also popping out to Paisley whenever I was in Glasgow just to look at Graham's immaculate fleet, now it seemed Fleetline dominated. Between trains more or less I nipped over to Dunoon, and another time fitted in Garelochhead. The Garelochhead fleet looked good, very good in fact, and has vanished without trace; that of Cowal Motor Services, successor to perhaps a dozen former operators, some of whom undoubtedly had new buses, yielded much less to enthuse about, but in some form it has endured.

So far Tayside had not figured in any of my itineraries; this omission was rectified in 1967. SBG let me down by late running into Perth, although if I had followed the crowd instead of staying on to the terminus I could have caught McLennan's bus to Dundee. As it was, the ex-Birmingham double decker – a Daimler? – waiting at their picking up point, was bound only for Errol, so I spent some time, by invitation of course, in the signal box there awaiting the next train to Dundee. Trains, and their associated fixtures, do sometimes come in handy, even on bus tours. Once there, at Broughty Ferry actually, I could spend a day out, with some assistance from Alexanders, sampling the services of Greyhound, Arbroath, and Mitchells of Luthermuir.

Moving forward by yet another decade, during which journeys north, though remaining enjoyable, provided little new to write about, I will linger over what was, when I started to write this article, my last. Disembarking at Stromness the night before, I had been surprised to find that buses there did not

*Left:* **Guy Arabs were once very common in the yellow-painted fleet of Graham's, Paisley. This 1957 Arab IV with Northern Counties 60-seat body is seen at Paisley Cross.** *Gavin Booth*

*Right:* **On the beautiful island of Arran, off Scotland's south-west coast, a Bedford YRT with Plaxton body in the fleet of Arran Coaches.** *Alan Millar*

wait for boats; I could have had a lift with a friendly wedding party, forgathering in Kirkwall from all parts of Scotland and well beyond, who had chartered a bus for this last leg, but decided that would be cheating. Waiting for the next one on genuine public service I was amply rewarded for my scruples; the middle-aged driver was a joy, friendly, humorous, and relaxed, making the sixteen mile journey something to savour. 'Travel with Peace' seemed a most appropriate slogan.

Next morning was rather different. Although the bus – this one really was meant to connect with the *St Ola* – came almost past my hotel, my friendly driver of the night before had advised me not to wait there, and not even to go to the bus station – a bus station in Kirkwall! – but to catch it at the garage. This was good advice. I was one of perhaps a dozen, including a sulky looking youth sprawled across the front seat, when we pulled into the bus station. Through steamy windows one could see a varied collection of greyish weatherbeaten hulks of buses, bringing to mind the German High Seas Fleet sunk nearby in Scapa Flow, and a waiting crowd, more than enough for our Plaxton-bodied Ford. It was the same bus I had enjoyed riding in the night before, but the driver, looking much the same, couldn't have been more different. Terse, irritable, aggressive, he seemed to be trying to tell somebody something.

Eventually, with comments becoming sharper, the sulky youth got up, out, and into the driving seat of one of the nearby battleships, the people remaining outside our bus following him. Did he pick up en route? Oh no; that was our job. Lost time couldn't be made up, no matter how hard our driver tried, and when we reached the quay at Stromness the ramp was up on *St Ola* and the crew were poised, waiting to cast off; within seconds we were under way.

This was the beginning of a time-consuming journey, varied, tiring, and perhaps best enjoyed in retrospect. It went bus / boat / bus / train / train (sleeper) / train / bus / bus / train / train / train / train / train / bus. There was time to eat well and to visit the theatre in Inverness, a puerile play but a fine theatre in a superb situation, before carrying on southwards.

All was peaceful at Queen Street next morning, and the sleeping car attendant, always courteous, no more hurried than usual, but on reaching Central there were queues to almost everywhere – how foolish I had been to choose the start of Glasgow's September holidays to arrive there. This, however, gave me an excuse. I might not be back for some time, if at all, and some of them might have vanished by then – I had bus operators in mind and not queuers – so why not have another quick trip to Paisley, Grahams, Cunninghams, and Patons, if not McGills. This included walking back a mile or so from Renfrew searching for Paton's bus to Govan – a few Scots must have thought me daft, not getting the bus there in front of me. Sure enough, two members of that surviving quartet vanished soon afterwards.

That excursion was made some five years ago. Independents aren't burgeoning in Scotland like they are in some parts of England, and anyway, new independents, with no PLSCs, Chevrolets, Reos or Regals, not to mention native Albions, Beardmores, or Halleys, in their ancestry lack glamour, but another exhilarating ride over Carter Bar and swooping down to Jedburgh would be a grand prelude to another part of the nine-tenths (at least) of Scotland as yet unseen.

The reality, coming when this account was nearly complete, was very different. Other compulsions, but still connected with buses, led me to Scotland again in May of 1983. Glasgow was the venue, but an extra day spent on the journey allowed a trip to Arran to be added on. Organisation of transport on the island, now in the hands of a single operator – why didn't I skip the boat at Lochranza when there were still half a dozen? – with the choice of a northern circular trip, a southern ditto, or all round

ROUND ARRAN
NSJ 200M

*Left:* **An unexpected sight in deepest Strathclyde – the Leyland National 2 in the fleet of Paterson, Dalry.** *Stewart J. Brown*

*Right:* **Many of the earliest rear-engined double-deckers had basically box-like bodywork, as on this 1959 Leyland Atlantean PDR1/1 with MCW 76-seat body in the Devon General fleet.** *T.W. Moore*

the island, by service bus in each case, merits longer description than I can give it here, and so does the fleet, so I will take up the story again at Ardrossan on the way back.

Reaching there again at 14.50, perhaps I should have managed a trip all the way to Glasgow by the new service of Bennetts if I had known about it, but I didn't, and my sights were fixed on something else involving the use of railway trains – the bus enthusiast should never scorn the iron rails as a means to an end.

A rush through the town to catch an earlier train at South Beach might have been less frustrating, but the waiting train at Harbour Station was too tempting; the only snag was the uneven headway, resulting in a 73 minutes wait in Kilwinning. Why does one always want to travel in the middle of the biggest time gap? Kilwinning on a hot, thundery day, with the main street looking like an open cast mining site, would have been a dead loss but for the buses, greens of AA, blue/maroons of A1, and a sprinkling of dark red Westerns, coming through in almost continuous procession.

I tore myself away to be in good time for the train to Glengarnock, finding temporary distraction in a post-wedding going away scene, but this couldn't prevent internal tension building up. Timing was fine. Alight Glengarnock 16.54, catch bus to Beith 16.56. Return without alighting, arriving Glengarnock 17.09 with plenty of time for a 17.20 train for Glasgow. I reassured myself with statistics seen on my local station – 95% of trains ran less than five minutes late. How foolish of me to pick that five per cent so often; it seemed my luck was out yet again.

Of course it came in the end, with nobody exhibiting any signs of impatience, worse still no signs of haste either, at Kilwinning or Dalry, so apart from re-checking Thomas Paterson and Brown's timetable every half minute and printing the OS map on my mind, neither did I. Alighting at Glengarnock, a few dignified steps took me out into the street, and a quick look at the bus stop across, devoid of people, seemed to confirm my fears. A quick change of plan, and I headed for the stop on my side for a return trip in the other direction to Kilbirnie, reconciling myself to a much later arrival in Glasgow.

Then it all happened. A familiar roar, and round the bend appeared a Leyland National in NBC red, perhaps a bit weatherbeaten NBC red (more like Lancashire United red really) and a three digit route number. No interest to me, but then, the classic delayed reaction. There should not be any NBC red in Scotland, and anyway the destination blind read 'BEITH SCHEME' or Beith something. A hurried wave to the driver, dart aross the street, and in. The train had arrived 10 minutes late, but the bus was 9 minutes late too, so two minutes had become not minus 8 but one. Nationals always sound impatient – it's that fan at the back really – but this was impatience plus. Over the railway, up the hill, round a big fast roundabout, through a short, quiet residential stretch of road, to unload in the centre of Beith. Beyond, to swing round another roundabout, rapid load again, then a swooping return. LCS317W had made up no time at all, but that still gave me two minutes even if the train was on time. It wasn't, of course.

People of Beith and of Kilbirnie have other ways of reaching Glasgow and the coast, but those who prefer the train are obviously well served for the first (bus) legs of their journeys by Mr Brown and Mr Paterson.

And what about John o'Groats? I did get there in the end with another quick dash on a spare day, but the weather, Torquay-like, warm, sunny, and windless as I was waiting in Wick for Mr Dunnet's very urban looking Bedford and as we rode for miles along the east coast, the terrain, flat and featureless, and most of all the bus load, young holidaymakers from all over Europe, America too, with hardly a Scots accent audible, made it a most 'un-Scottish' occasion.

# Double-Deck Bodies an Architectural Guide

GAVIN BOOTH

How can I classify double-deck bodies, I asked myself when researching the Leyland Atlantean book (buy now while stocks last!). Not so easy, I found, until a book on architecture pointed towards similarities. Can bus bodies be described as Romanesque? Or Baroque? Or even Brutalist? You may not agree, but it's an interesting thought. So here's a slightly tongue-in-cheek attempt to apply architectural classifications to more mundane and less permanent structures.

00
Greater Manchester Transport
5002

13
Town Centre
Westcliffe Road
AINSDALE BEACH
82
VWM 82L
JOHNS

*Above left:* **The near-equal side window spacing on the MCW Metrobus is well demonstrated on this Greater Manchester example.** *R. Moore*

*Left:* **The infinitely adaptable Alexander AL-type body, here with front and rear peaks, flat screens and short side windows, in the Southport Corporation fleet in pre-Merseyside PTE days.** *A.L. Such*

*Above:* **The use of standard Routemaster parts meant that the unique rear-engined example, FRM1, was a competent and well-proportioned bus.** *Gavin Booth*

*Right:* **Alexander played its part in the Renaissance of body design with its early 1960s styles that made imaginative use of glassfibre and curved glass. The less common lowheight D-type is seen on a Daimler Fleetline of Graham's of Paisley, previously with A1, Ardrossan.** *Gavin Booth*

**Romanesque** architecture is earth-bound, made up of simple geometric forms. Much the same could be said of the very earliest bodies on rear-engined double-deckers. MCW set a pattern in 1956 with its body for prototype Leyland Atlantean 281 ATC, producing an essentially box-like shape incorporating elements of the current MCW Orion body. The production Atlanteans that followed in 1958 were largely similar, but now the engine compartment was a feature of the design, with the prominent 'boot' behind the rear axle; on 281 ATC the engine and gearbox were contained within the integrally-constructed body shell, and this ensured a clean rear profile.

These first bodies on production Atlanteans were built in both normal height and semi-lowbridge forms, but while they attracted great attention because of their novelty value, the bodies were far from beautiful. Body design on traditional front-engined chassis was going through an awkward stage at the time, and the family resemblance to the Orion did not help.

The Atlantean was an opportunity for bodybuilders to produce something startlingly different, but for a few years none did. Early Alexander-bodied Atlanteans were similar to the MCW product, with a more curvaceous front dome to relieve the bland lines. Roe, which at one time could always be counted on to produce something shapely and well-proportioned, actually managed to build bodies that were considerably *uglier* than the MCW products. Northern Counties, a coachbuilder with a good eye for proportion, successfully adapted its standard body for one of the first production lowheight Daimler Fleetlines in 1961, and was the first builder to deal satisfactorily with the rear 'bustle', by fitting fairings above the engine compartment to ensure a smoother profile.

In spite of developments in double-deck body design, which will be covered under other headings, some builders continued to churn out Romanesque bodies for many years. Not that they were all bad. There *were* the bad ones of course: Massey produced a disappointingly angular design in 1964. Park Royal's first bodies on rear-engined double-decks, in 1962, were surprisingly like the contemporary MCW product, and many were frustrated when this design was specified for London Transport's experimental Atlanteans and Fleetlines in 1965. LT's only home-made rear-engined double-decker, FRM1 the 1966 rear-engined Routemaster, was considerably more successful, incorporating as it did a large percentage of normal RM parts, which at least meant good proportions and close attention to detail.

The longest-running Romanesque body style was probably that built by Eastern Coach Works. Unmistakeably a Lowestoft design, with standard ECW glazing, the body was competent if unexciting, particularly in lowheight form on Bristol VRT or Daimler Fleetline chassis; when 'stretched' to normal height the body never looked quite so comfortable.

---

**Renaissance** architecture represented revival, not rebirth, a look back to the classical age. Applied to bus bodies it covers the period from 1962 when operators and bodybuilders came to terms with the rear-engined double-decker, and realised that looks were important after all. In some ways this was a return to the days of bespoke municipal designs, so we suddenly had clearly different Glasgow, Liverpool and Sheffield Atlanteans, for instance.

The Glasgow Atlanteans, bodied by Alexander, were a clever adaptation of the basic body structure to provide double-curvature upper and lower front screens. These produced a successfully different design that was widely imitated – by Roe and Weymann in particular. As often happens the original was by far the most successful.

Liverpool Corporation and MCW worked together to develop a style with sharp contemporary lines, featuring peaked domes and a laudable attention to design detail. Features of this design were adopted by other builders, and in many ways the current East Lancs design (which first appeared in 1963 for Bolton) still has Liverpudlian echoes.

For Sheffield, Park Royal took its basic body and grafted on sharp new front-end styling; Roe did something similar for Oldham. These were simple yet successful cosmetic changes. Roe also produced a peak-dome body for Sunderland, while Willowbrook's first bodies on rear-engined double-deck were Atlanteans for Coventry with a style that was refreshingly different.

Not all of the big municipal operators sought individuality. Birmingham took a rather bland version of the Park Royal standard body, and Manchester took the MCW standard with a rather nasty flat windscreen.

But the Renaissance movement was an important one. Although the basic five-bay window layout of early Atlanteans remained, there was a clear desire to tidy up at least the front end, and produce buses that *looked* different to prospective passengers. Even ECW, always the most conservative of coachbuilders, grafted a peaked dome on to its standard body (on Atlanteans for Colchester and Fleetlines for South Yorkshire PTE), but with limited success: mutton dressed as lamb?

**Baroque** architecture relies heavily on theatrical effect, and bus bodies in this category include designs for operators with highly individual views on bus body design. Nottingham City Transport produced its own decidedly 'different' styling, featuring a front end profile that was a mass of apparently competing angles. East Lancs, MCW, Northern Counties and Willowbrook were persuaded to build variations on this theme, and very soon a clear Nottingham design emerged.

In Ireland, CIE moved from very traditional bus bodies on Leyland Titan PD3 to an amazingly angular design on its first Atlanteans. Built by CIE on Metal Sections frames, CIE's Atlanteans were unlike anything that has – thankfully – been seen since. At least until the appearance in 1980 of the prototype Bombardier double-deck, designed and built for CIE. Part of a family of similar buses and coaches, the visual theme of the Bombardier single-deckers is echoed in the double-deckers, resulting in a distinctive if uneasy body.

More successful, to my mind at least, was the body built in 1978 for Nottingham by Northern Counties, with sharp lines that acted as a reminder of the earlier Nottingham 'specials'.

---

**The Gothic Revival** in architecture was, according to my researches, 'the symbol of the lost innocence of the middle ages'. Applied (very) loosely to bus bodies this could be seen as the period when the Renaissance designs were consolidated. Side window bay lengths no longer owed much to the 1958 prototype Atlanteans. Windows became longer – up to 2.3 metres long on Alexander bodies – and bodybuilders took a fresh look at the shape of the double-deck bus, particularly now that it could be 10 metres long.

Roe developed a series of well-proportioned long-windowed 10 metre bodies for Leeds City Transport from 1968.

Alexander produced the infinitely adaptable AL type in 1972, available with peaks or rounded domes, flat or curved front screens, with panoramic or normal-length side windows, with engine fairings or not. Although the Alexander peaked domes were fashionable, if rather overdone, the AL type was successful in its many different guises.

**The disappointingly square Massey body, here on Leyland Atlantean PDR1/1 chassis for Colchester Corporation, new in 1968.** *G.R. Mills*

*Left:* **East Lancs body designs have not changed greatly over the years, and many municipal fleets operate Leyland Atlanteans similar to this 1977 AN68A/1R in the unusual blue and red livery of Hyndburn.** *Gavin Booth*

*Below:* **Baroque perhaps, but certainly distinctive – the angular bodywork for the first of CIE's D-class Atlanteans was built by CIE on Metal Sections frames.** *Gavin Booth*

*Right:* **The happiest version of the ubiquitous '1970s standard' body was built by Northern Counties for Selnec and Greater Manchester, although this 1977 Daimler Fleetline FE30AGR was actually built for the associated Lancashire United fleet. It is seen in the revised livery which further enhances the design.** *John Robinson*

SCHOOL SERVICE
Alarm Fitted
SN
490
OBN 507R

**Art Nouveau**, a stylised if sometimes extravagant movement, paved the way for more recent architectural styles. The nearest bus equivalents were those design that were regarded as revolutionary in their time, and yet have since come to be recognised as trend-setters; well, most of them.

The Park Royal (later East Lancs, MCW and Roe) body for Manchester Corporation, the Mancunian, is the best example. Conceived from the outset as a one-man double-decker, the Mancunian body defied the existing design conventions. The ultra-deep front windscreens, the subtly square lines, the long side windows – all have their echoes in more recent bodies.

Unrestrained by history, Van Hool McArdle in Ireland produced a dramatic body style when it won an order from South Yorkshire PTE. Its most distinctive feature, the extra-deep front upstairs screen, is still with us on the Alexander R-type body.

There were other, smaller batches of pure Art Nouveau bodies, like the Bolton Atlanteans with East Lancs bodies that featured forward-sloping window pillars.

---

**Brutalism** in architecture is the 'warts and all' movement that produces buildings that are a mass of material and undisguised surfaces. In bus terms it seems appropriate to include those bodies that made it to the metal in defiance of all design considerations. The most notable was the single double-deck body built by Fowler on Atlantean chassis for Fishwick of Leyland; praiseworthy in view of the limited resources available to the bodybuilders, it represents an all-time low in design terms. Less excusable were the 30 Atlanteans built in 1978 for Tyne & Wear PTE by Willowbrook, which tend to look as if they had been built from available stock parts, without any real thought to appearance. Poor Willowbrook might also creep into this category with the bodies built in 1976-80 for NBC fleets, Merseywide PTE and Cardiff. These were based on an admirable design, but lacked much of its original subtlety.

**Modern** is the catch-all term for contemporary architecture, both good and bad. Fortunately most bus bodies falling into this category have been good, as builders and operators recognised the importance of good design, and came to terms – at last – with the rear-engined double-decker.

Spearheading the Modern movement was a design built by Park Royal in 1968 on 10 metre Atlanteans for Plymouth and Sheffield, and then in 1969 on 9.5 metre Fleetlines for East Kent. The East Kent variation was to be the forerunner of many thousands of largely similar buses. Eschewing definite peaks for a squarer dome, and opting for longer-than-normal (1.6 metre pillar centres) side windows, Park Royal produced a body style that looked good in 9.5 and 10 metre lengths.

An important break from tradition was the general window spacing on 9.5 metre buses. From 1958 double-deckers had usually had five main side windows (five bays) more or less equating to the area from ahead of the front axle to behind the rear axle. ECW had challenged this trend in 1968 with its first bodies on Bristol VRT; it still provided five windows, but they extended towards the rear, and the last side window was very small, a tradition carried forward from the Bristol FLF Lodekka body, but on a rear-engined chassis equating with the size of the engine compartment. The 1968 Park Royal body opted for four bays in this area, to ECW's five, again with a very small last side window. This was the case on 9.5 metre bodies; on 10 metre bodies the extra length was reflected in a longer last side window. This did not mean the end of the five-bay layout, for Alexander, East Lancs and ECW stuck to it for another decade.

The basic lines were picked up by other builders – MCW, Northern Counties, Roe – and the '1970s standard' body was born. Here was a body whose lines were right, and which could still give operators the individuality they sought. Selnec/Greater Manchester used it to best effect with its standard body styles, built by Northern Counties and Park Royal. West Midlands PTE used it less successfully, while London Transport's once large Fleetline fleet had a Londonised version with oversquare roof edges. National Bus evolved its own variant, which was built by Park Royal and Roe for a number of NBC fleets. Marshall opted for this general window layout in 1980 when it built its first ever double-deck bodies, although with a distinct inward curve towards the roof, which aids instant recognition, something that could be awkward with the other bodies.

MCW started a further trend in 1973 with the appearance of the integral Metropolitan double-decker. Although at first glance similar to the '1970s standard', it was in fact subtly different. Not just the asymetric windscreens that were an instantly recognisable trade mark, but the general approach to window spacing which meant a reversion to the four-bay layout, with similar size windows above the passenger door and behind the rear axle. This set a trend that has since been widely imitated. Leyland's B15 (later Titan) had similar window spacing, but with extra-deep lower deck windows. MCW's Metrobus (1977) followed suit, as did the Alexander R-type (1980), ECW/Roe bodies on Olympian (1980), and East Lancs and Marshall.

The next changes to the appearance of double-deck bodies may well come from a wider acceptance of fixed direct glazing, similar to many modern coaches. Some bodies have already been built with this type of glazing, most notably by East Lancs, and it seems likely that other builders will follow as the technique is perfected. In terms of appearance, direct glazing permits much smoother lines, without the heavy window rubbers that are necessary on most bodies.

*Left:* **A bold approach to double-deck styling, the Northern Counties-bodied Leyland Atlantean built for Nottingham in 1978.** *T.W. Moore*

*Right:* **Effective and simple changes alter the appearance of this Leyland Atlantean AN68A/2R with East Lancs body, in the Lancaster fleet.** *Michael Dryhurst*

*Left:* **MCW's design for the Metropolitan was further developed when the Metrobus model appeared. One of London's first Metrobuses, M36, shows the asymetrical windscreen arrangement that was a feature of the Mk 1 version.** *J.P. Orr*

*Below:* **The extra length and low overall height of Reading's 10metre Bristol VRTs affects the appearance of the Northern Counties bodywork. Fifty of these 'Jumbos' were bought between 1971 and 1976.** *M.J. Russell*

*Right:* **The Van Hool-McArdle bodies for South Yorkshire PTE on Volvo Ailsa underframes looked strange in 1976, but anticipated some more recent trends. Two similar buses went to A1, Ardrossan in 1977, and one is seen at Kilmarnock bus station.** *Gavin Booth*

*Below right:* **The Leyland-designed bodywork for the integral Titan model introduced a look that continued with ECW and Roe bodies on Olympian, but without the distinctive extra-deep lower deck windows. This Titan demonstrator was working for Brighton in 1983.** *Gavin Booth*

A1
ARDROSSAN
ALSERVICE
PSJ 824R

27
Brighton Station
Leyland
VAO 488Y

# Taken Over: 1

**The take-over of smaller bus fleets by company, municipal or PTE undertakings often results in some decidedly non-standard vehicles appearing in familiar liveries, albeit for only a brief period in some cases. Here and elsewhere in the *Annual* are photographs of some of the interesting buses taken over during the last quarter century.**

*Left:* **The 1963 take-over of Silver Star, Porton Down, brought coaches like this Leyland Tiger Cub/Harrington into the all-Bristol Wilts & Dorset fleet.** *G.R. Mills*

*Below:* **A Park Royal-bodied Leyland Leopard taken over in 1969 by United Counties with part of the famous Birch Bros. business.** *G.R. Mills*

*Right:* **Luton was one of the few Corporation fleets to pass into other hands. This Leyland Lowlander with East Lancs body went with the undertaking to United Counties in 1970.** *G.R. Mills*

*Below right:* **Equally rare are take-overs by municipal fleets. Tailby & George (Blue Bus Service) of Willington was acquired by Derby Corporation in 1973; an ex-Blue Bus Daimler Fleetline/Northern Counties in 1975.** *G.R. Mills*

STOPSLEY (CROWLAND ROAD)
45 SERVICE
HIRE-A-VAN (LUTON) LTD.
5cwt - 5ton
UNITED COUNTIES
177 HTM

BURTON
VIA REPTON
DERBY
25
325 YNU

# Southdown at Seventy

**Looking back with D. FEREDAY GLENN**

Anniversaries are always a good time for taking stock. For the occasion of its Golden Jubilee in 1965, Southdown produced a most readable account of the first fifty years; however, much of significance has taken place since then, so it may not come amiss to look back again over the seven decades at some milestones and noteworthy vehicles that have emerged in the career of 'SMS'.

Although Southdown itself was incorporated on June 2, 1915, it did not appear as a new phenomenon overnight, but was rather the pragmatic amalgam in time of war of three rival factions — Worthing Motor Services, London & South Coast Haulage Company and the country services of the Brighton, Hove & Preston United Omnibus Company. Even then, the earliest pioneer and forerunner of Worthing Motor Services had been Sussex Motor Road Car Company with a route between the coastal town and Pulborough in 1904! The founding of Southdown Motor Services Ltd yielded a fleet of 31 highly assorted buses, although some were dubbed charabancs because of single-deck bodywork with individual doors along the side for access. All, needless to say, were on solid tyres!

But there was little time for complacency in the early days: new operators, often with no more than one or two small vehicles, were setting up in business as fast as they could obtain licences to run them. Flair and adaptability were necessary virtues for pioneering crews, as clearly emerges from anecdotes of the period. If the 'cradle' of Southdown was in the Sussex coastal towns of Worthing and Brighton, its territory was quickly extended to east and west with routes to Lewes and right along the shoreline to Portsmouth. The cut and thrust of competition (before the Road Traffic Act of 1930 brought a more ordered system) resulted in much ingenuity to outflank the opposition; the outcome in many instances was amalgamation or outright purchase. Even beyond

its own recognised boundaries, Southdown was pursuing a policy of co-operation with other firmly established companies, which had the same directors on the board of each. Thus joint services were begun with Hants & Dorset, Aldershot & District, Maidstone & District and East Kent Road Car Company Ltd in the years immediately after the Armistice. Associations were forged with influential organisations such as the British Electric Traction group, a link that was to remain in being until 1968.

Technical innovations were appearing thick and fast, too. Once pneumatic tyres became standard equipment for buses in about 1926, the tremendous variety and quaint features of the pioneer vehicles began to give way to greater orthodoxy and standardisation. Relatively modern charabancs of the 1920s were rebuilt with the new tyres and open-top double-deck bodywork for a fresh lease of life but, by 1929, the arrival of the Leyland Titan chassis with servo-assisted brakes, six cylinder engine and a dropped frame that would allow the construction of covered-top bodywork signalled the beginning of a new era. Improved roads coupled with the new design meant that coach holidays and express services could be greatly extended and developed: 'all-weather' tourers gave way to sliding roofs and curved glass panels to improve the view, while the long-bonneted normal control design was steadily displaced by the higher-capacity forward control vehicle. Fuel consumption began to be a factor to be considered and diesel-engined buses made an appearance in 1934. There was also a brief flirtation with 'gearless' buses having torque-convertor transmission, but these were rebuilt with conventional gearboxes soon after the ending of World War 2. Coaches persisted with petrol engines for somewhat longer as they were considered quieter, but by 1939 diesels had become the norm. So rapid were the technical and styling improvements that vehicles less than ten years old were being sold off long before they were life-expired. Indeed, a wellknown Titan TD1 now happily preserved was sold in 1938 – a mere eight years old – to be used in Scotland for a further 14 years in service, virtually in original condition, because technical advances and a new fleet of diesel buses had rendered it surplus to Southdown's needs.

The onset of war soon brought production of buses to a halt; fuel rationing created a captive market. A large number of single-deck buses and coaches was requisitioned for the war effort and

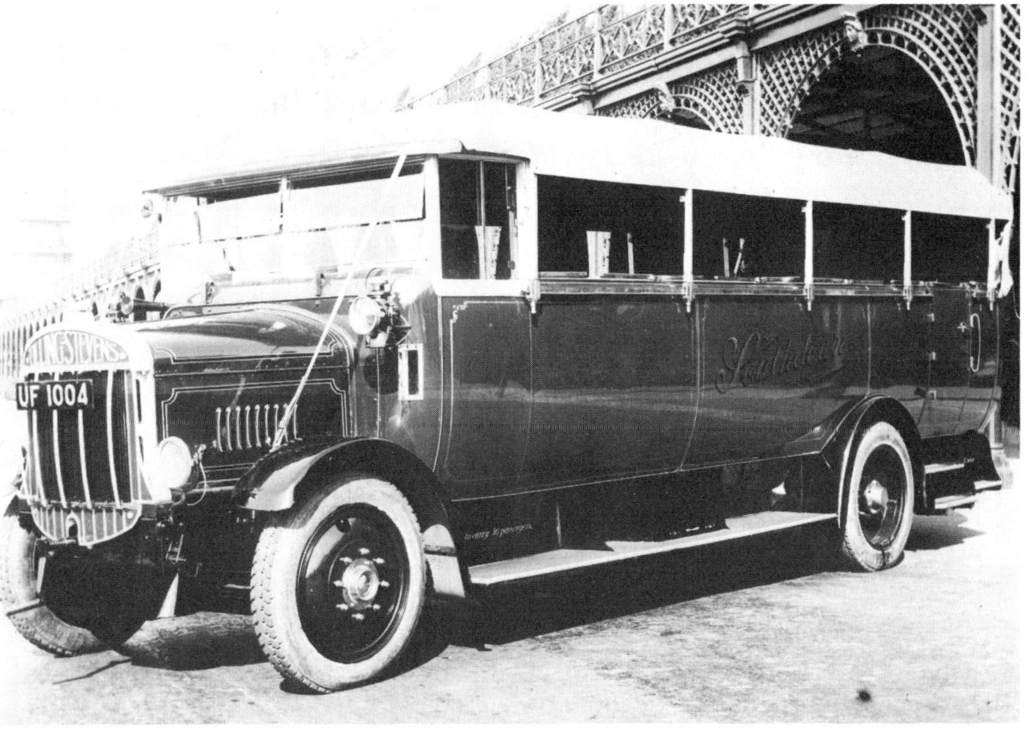


*Left:* **One of the earliest Southdown buses, a Milnes-Daimler acquired from Worthing Motor Services, and seen in Worthing about 1910.** *Southdown*

*Above:* **New at Brighton in 1926, Tilling-Stevens B9B no. 409 with its original Harrington charabanc body was one of the first Southdown buses delivered with pneumatic tyres.** *Southdown*

forces' transport, so there was a sudden shortage of vehicles to do the work. All remaining petrol-engined double-deckers were reprieved for the duration: the 23 open-top Brush-bodied Leyland Titan TD1 vehicles delivered in 1929 were equipped with a hideous temporary canvas roof to enable them to be used in all weathers, while the remaining covered-top TD1 and TD2 buses were sent to an assortment of coachbuilders for rebodying in utility style. But this was not enough, and 100 Guy Arab double-deckers with various kinds of austerity bodywork and 5- or 6-cylinder Gardner diesel engines joined the fleet in 1943-5. Elderly petrol coaches were employed on ambulance duties, and many of the splendid 1400 series Leyland Tiger single-deck buses were modified with perimeter seating to carry 50 or 60 passengers in comparative discomfort instead of 32 in accustomed luxury! Grey roofs were applied on repainting, while some of the Guys were delivered in all-grey livery with wood slatted seats and no glazed upper-deck rear windows! It was a far cry from the expansive days of the 1930s . . .

When the dark days of war were over, it was remarkable how quickly some of the old standards were reinstated. With petrol rationing still in force for private motorists, the buses had a field day. Routes restricted or withdrawn during hostilities, for some were close to sensitive defence establishments, airfields or beaches, were soon operational again and – pending sufficient supplies of paint to restore them to cream – green roofs replaced the sombre wartime grey on double-deckers. A major programme of rebuilding the bulk of prewar double-deckers with new bodies improved the condition of the existing fleet while slow deliveries of new vehicles began to appear in 1946. The first postwar double-deckers retained the utilitarian style in appearance, but the war-tested 7.4 litre diesel engines were very economical; Southdown received 50 of the Leyland Titan PD1 models and more than double that number of similar-engined Tiger PS1 coaches to bolster the express and excursion traffic. Eighty of the famous PD2 model double-deckers, all with Leyland bodies, entered service in 1948 together with a dozen more Guys with 6LW units – all without any reduction in the numbers of prewar vehicles still in service! Route extensions followed, and a temporary arrangement with Portsmouth Corporation for the war period blossomed into a full-scale Joint Agreement for the area. In summer several of the original Brush-bodied TD1s reverted to open-top for sea front duties at Brighton, Worthing and Hayling Island; everyone wanted to travel by bus.

Not until 1950 was it necessary to dispense with any of the older vehicles. With new deliveries coming thick and fast, at last the fleet was up to strength again. New legislation allowed for wider

*Above:* **One of the smaller vehicles delivered in 1936 was Leyland Cub KP3A no. 15, with 20-seat Park Royal bodywork for country duties on narrow roads.** *Southdown*

*Right:* **Also from 1936 were six superb Leyland Tigress touring coaches with luxury 20-seat Burlingham bodies. The glass roof panels and electrically-operated hood were fitted to 319 when new.** *Southdown*

*Right:* **Purely functional in appearance, the wartime Guy Arabs were extremely useful. This was one of the few to have Strachans utility bodywork and Gardner 6LW engine on delivery in 1944.** *Southdown*

*Left:* **One of the final batch of petrol-engined double-deckers delivered in 1936, this Leyland Titan with Beadle 52-seat lowbridge body had been fitted with an 8.6 litre diesel when seen at Petersfield in the late 1940s.** *D. Clark*

*Left:* **At Selby bus station, a Bedford YRT with Duple body in the fleet of Jaronda Travel of Barlow.** *M. Fowler*

*Below:* **One of the best-known private coach businesses in Britain, Yelloway of Rochdale, and a Plaxton-bodied 12metre Leyland Leopard ready for an express service to Blackpool.** *G. Coxon*

*Right:* **With Durham Castle as a backdrop, a Duple Dominant-bodied Bedford YMT in the fleet of Langley Park Motor Co, better known as Gypsy Queen.** *G. Coxon*

# Independent Colour

DURHAM
VIA WITTON GILBERT
& EARLS HOUSE HOSP.
GYPSY QUEEN SERVICE 53
Gypsy Queen
GYPSY QUEEN
APT 582S

and longer vehicles, so the next batch of Leyland PD2 double-deckers measured 27ft long by 8ft wide; meanwhile the first generation of underfloor-engined coaches and single-deckers with full-fronted bodies was beginning to cause a stir. The last petrol-engined buses and coaches to be purchased, thanks to the restrictions of weight imposed by the bridge between Havant and Hayling Island, comprised ten Dennis Falcon single-deckers and a brace of Duple-bodied Bedfords to assist with express and excursion duties. Just as 1929/30 had marked a watershed in vehicle development between the wars, so 1950 was a similar 'vintage year'. The Hayling Bridge was rebuilt in 1956.

If coach development was advancing quickly and producing a new generation of styles, double-deck buses remained very traditional with more Leyland PD2s and a further delivery of Guys; the latter were particularly associated with the eastern area and gave sterling service on hilly routes in East Sussex, especially between Eastbourne and Brighton. It was not until 1957 that the first full-fronted double-deckers appeared, being lengthened to 30ft. No less than 285 of the Leyland PD3 design were to be taken into stock in the succeeding ten years, a remarkable measure of standardisation. Single-deck chassis became standardised on first the Leyland Royal Tiger, then the Tiger Cub and finally the Leopard, the last-named with bodies up to 36ft in length. Although the coach fleet followed much the same pattern, there was an unusual innovation with Commer chassis utilising a 3-cylinder two-stroke engine of great economy. The first 25 featured Beadle coachwork and were always associated with the South Coast Express duties between Margate and Bournemouth, while later vehicles were bodied both by Burlingham and Harrington.

The last prewar vehicles in public service were withdrawn in the early 1960s, some having given more than 20 years' use to the company. The last of the utility Guys went in 1964, many having been rebuilt to open-top as successors to the petrol Titans on sea front duties. The loss of passengers through competition from the private car forced economies to be made: some routes in rural areas were abandoned or amalgamated and simplification of the traditional livery was made possible by the modern bodywork designs. With the closure of some of its long-standing coachbuilders, Southdown had to rely on Duple and Plaxton for most of its coaches, although loss of individuality was somehow staunched by imaginative use of traditional paint schemes. As if in anticipation of the sale of its omnibus interests by the British Electric Traction group in 1969, Southdown ordered its first Bristol RE chassis for single-deck buses in 1968, while a last display of individuality came with an order for 30 dual-purpose Leyland Leopard vehicles with distinctive bodywork by

Northern Counties.

Amalgamation with the former Tilling fleet of Brighton, Hove & District came on January 1, 1969 and Southdown became a constituent of the National Bus Company network. The last coaches to be delivered in the famous livery were the UUF-J series in 1971, while new Bristol VRT double-deckers with rear engines (as well as some Daimler Fleetlines) concluded the green and cream paint style in 1972; thereafter National green and white was the order of the day, with coaches in plain white. There followed a rather sad period of mediocrity, relieved only by the re-emergence for psv use on special duties of the company's preserved 1929 petrol Titan TD1 No 813 in all its glory. The 1922-vintage Leyland G7 with 1928 Short Bros. open-top body sold to Provincial in 1935 was retrieved in 1970, being restored to similar pristine condition by 1972 for publicity purposes at Rallies.

In 1981 two of the UUF-J coaches were restored to their original livery for local coach duties; the scheme was so popular that others of the same batch have followed. More recently the 'Sussex Link' express duties have been heralded by a colourful adaptation of the traditional colours, and some limited stop services with double-deckers have provided an excuse for a brighter livery using yellow panels between the decks. The latest Leyland Tiger coaches (Nos 1001-1005) display an imaginative combination of old and new colours worthy of their 1930 predecessors (Tiger TS2) that were allocated the same fleet numbers. Southdown at 70 is alive and well!

*Left:* **This 1970 view illustrates the change in the Southdown double-deck fleet in the late 1950s. Leading is the fleet's final Guy Arab/Park Royal, dating from 1956, and in the rear one of the fleet of Leyland PD3s.** *D. Fereday Glenn*

*Right:* **A reminder of the Steine Street premises, occupied by Southdown from the very beginning until 1964, Here a 1963 Leyland Leopard with Weymann Castilian bodywork squeezes from the depot.** *Southdown*

*Below:* **Latest in a long line of coaches, a Leyland Tiger with Plaxton bodywork displays a variation of the NBC livery, using dark green and gold.** *D. Fereday Glenn*

# The Saro Story

**GEOFF COXON on the brief but influential life of Saunders-Roe**

The origin of this once diversified company dates back to 1830. Moses Saunders, who helped to construct weirs and locks on the River Thames, progressed to boat-building under the name of S. E. Saunders Ltd and then into aircraft building, in particular flying boats. In 1928, Sir Alliott Verdon-Roe took a financial interest in the company, and it was consequently renamed Saunders-Roe Ltd. In 1937, Saunders Shipyards Ltd was formed as an associated company to concentrate on the boat-building activities. The company became a major contractor to the Ministry of Defence and was kept extremely busy during World War 2. It was during this time that a new purpose-built factory was built on the shores of the Menai Straits at Beaumaris, North Wales to concentrate on the conversion and maintenance of wartime Catalina flying boats. When the War ended, the company undertook to reorganise its widely dispersed collection of factories engaged on a variety of work, much of which had little application to peacetime needs. With plenty of spare capacity resulting from this reorganisation, the Beaumaris works was occupied by Saunders Shipyard Ltd, an associated company whose Cowes boat-building yard had been destroyed during the War. Although boat and small naval craft building was to continue to form a major part of the production at Beaumaris, moves were afoot to enter the transport bodywork sector, in particular bus bodies and large tanker bodies. Consequently the company's name was changed to Saunders Engineering and Shipyard Ltd (SEAS) and then again in 1951 when it was given the shortened title of Saunders-Roe (Anglesey) Ltd. This name existed until 1960 when the company was absorbed into the de Havilland Group.

The company had over many years

gathered a wealth of experience of various types of aircraft and marine construction built in light alloy; this retained strength and versatility compared with steel structures. It was with this in mind that Saunders decided to enter the bus bodybuilding market. With the return to peace in 1945, bus operators were faced with the prospects of replacing war-torn buses as soon as possible. It was reported in 1946 that Saunders was to commence bus bodybuilding under the managing directorship of Mr W. P. Kemp who had been closely connected with the manufacture of all-metal bus bodies with Short Bros (Rochester & Bedford) Ltd. The only road connection between Anglesey and the mainland was across the Menai Bridge and this had to be strengthened and modified to permit full-height double-deckers to cross over it.

During its first year, Saunders received an order from Southdown Motor Services. This was to rebuild a lowbridge Short-bodied Leyland Titan TD4 and a Harrington-bodied single-deck Leyland Tiger TS7. The first order for new vehicles came from Northern General which took delivery of 18 AEC Regal IIIs with 36-seat bus bodies, basically to the BET Federation standard design. They were composite bodies incorporating light alloy inserts, deep windows and flared skirt panels. Unfortunately by 1948/49, Northern had experienced trouble with roof drumming and some were returned for frame stiffening; the remainder were repaired by Northern. Further orders came from Southdown, this time to rebody four Leyland TD4s and three Leyland TD5s. These were all completed during 1947 and had H28/26R bodies. Also in 1947 a batch of Foden PVSC5 chassis was bodied, comprising two for Caerphilly Urban District Council, six for Crown Coaches, Birtley, six for Green Bus, Rugeley and one on a Foden PVSC6 for Salopia of Whitchurch. As well as the Fodens, a batch of Guy Arab Mk IIIs was bodied for independent operators. Notably two for Berresfords, Cheddleton, two for Mainwaring Brothers, Audley (acquired by PMT), three for Milton Bus Services Ltd (acquired by PMT), one for Beckett of Bucknall, one for Brown Bros, Sapcote and two for Vessey, Hibaldstow. They all had 'roomy' bodywork of composite construction.

Saunders' first export order was completed during 1947; these were 60 Guy Arab Mk IIIs, with 19ft6in wheelbase and Gardner 6LW engines. They were delivered to importers De Nederlandsle Motoren Maatschappij NV of Rotterdam and were distributed to various bus companies in the Netherlands. Many, however, were rebodied or rebuilt by Dutch bodybuilders. More interest developed nearer home in the form of deliveries to Midland General and Maidstone & District. Early in 1948, Midland General took delivery of 25 Leyland PSIs with attractively-styled bodywork, some with 35 bus seats and others with dual-purpose 32 seats and externally finished in typical Midland General chrome strip mouldings. Maidstone & District took delivery of a batch of 40 Bristol K6As with nicely-proportioned 56-seat bodies with flared skirt panels and a neat upper deck front rake.

With other types of work declining at Beaumaris, a vigorous and successful sales effort was carried out to keep the production lines busy. Valuable export orders were completed during 1948. There were 50 AEC Regal MK IIIs for Lisbon Electric Tramways – the chassis of which had drop rear ends and seated

*Top:* **One of the first Saunders contracts was for 18 AEC Regals for Northern General in 1946. They had 36-seat bodies built to BET specification, with deep windows.**

*Above:* **One of two Guy Arab III with SEAS 36-seat forward entrance bodywork delivered to South Notts in 1947.** *R. Marshall*

*Facing page:* **The classic lines of the best-remembered Saro body style are enhanced by the traditional blue and white Sunderland District livery on this 1954 Leyland Tiger Cub.** *G. Coxon*

*Above:* **Midland General took a batch of 25 Leyland Tiger PS1s with handsome Saunders bodies in 1948.** *G.H.F. Atkins*

24 passengers plus 12 standing on the rear platform and 9 standing on the front platform. 91 AEC Regal IIIs were delivered to Companhia de Transportes Colectivos of Sao Paulo, Brazil and extensive use of light alloy construction was used and the bodies incorporated a neat full front design. 20 Daimler chassis were delivered to Kumasi Municipal Transport of Ghana.

After the War London Transport was undertaking a major replacement programme of its war-worn fleet and as a result delivery of new buses did not keep pace with the withdrawal of old vehicles. In order to speed up the programme, London Transport ordered buses bodied by Saunders and Cravens which were non-standard in construction, although having some modifications to meet London Transport's requirements.

Between 1948 and 1950, 250 Saunders-bodied RT buses (RT 1152-1401) were built, and a further 50 were delivered in 1950-1951 (RT 4218-4267). The bodies were similar in appearance to the standard 3RT3 type with a roof number box, but the offside route number plate was placed further back. The Saunders bodies had a metal roof, whereas standard RT buses had a one-piece jicwood roof. The Saunders bodies incorporated lightweight aluminium cruciform construction and were not interchangeable with Park Royal and Weymann bodies. During their production, Saunders fell behind with delivery promises mainly due to a bottleneck in the paint shop and some of the batch were sub-contracted out for finishing into London Transport colours. It was recorded that maintenance was not so economical compared with Park Royal or Weymann bodied RTs, as structural spares had to be ordered specially for the 300 vehicles, which was small in comparison with the main RT fleet. However, after some initial minor problems, the Saunders-bodied RTs lasted as well as the other makes of bodywork on RT chassis. It was felt that London Transport was responsible for helping to raise the standards of Saunders bodywork at that time.

During 1948 the market place was becoming very competitive. Many of the large bus operators were demanding lighter, stronger, safer and quieter buses which would give long service life and would be more economical to operate. Many bodybuilders decided to produce an all metal body instead of a composite (metal/wood) body which had been the norm for such a long time. Many of the leading bodybuilders were using light alloy construction, such as Beadle, Harrington, Strachans and ECW, while others had settled for an all-steel construction, like Duple and Willowbrook. As well as satisfying the home market, several overseas markets would not entertain a composite body and to many bodybuilders, including Saunders, this was one market where large orders could be won. It was acknowledged that with a light alloy construction, considerable saving in weight could be achieved compared with a body of composite or steel construction. With less deadweight, it meant a greater payload, reduced fuel consumption and generally longer vehicle life. It was also considered to be much stronger as riveted joints gave enormous structural strength combined with the durability of non-corroding light alloy. It was also safer because of the lower centre of gravity and improved roadholding qualities. It was also quieter because there were no 'working' joints to creak and with greater rigidity the body was free from vibration and consequently gave a longer service life. However, one disadvantage of the all-alloy body was its higher initial cost compared with the composite or steel body.

In 1949 a repeat order was completed for Lisbon Electric Tramways, these being 10 AEC Regal Mk IIIs with similar bodies to the previous batch but supplied in CKD condition (completely knocked down) and assembled in LET's own workshops. While some of Northern's AEC Regals were being rectified at Beaumaris, a Leyland TS7 which originally had a Wycombe coach body was sent for rebodying and returned to Northern along with the repaired Regals. Apart from one rebodied Bristol K5G chassis for Maidstone & District in 1950 and the large batch for LTE subsequent bodies were to be constructed using a new all-lightweight alloy structure known as the Rivaloy body, the name originating from the method of securing the panels (rivets) to the structure (alloy).

Saunders set out to convince bus operators of the advantages of its new design. This enabled Saunders to achieve a world-wide reputation for its Rivaloy body and during the next 2-3 years it was able to win some large export orders.

The Rivaloy lightweight body was suitable for both single and double-deck chassis. Crosville took the first example in November 1949, a rebodied 1936 Leyland TS7 followed by another 13 which were completed by March 1950. They all had 35-seat rear entrance bodies and were locally known as 'battleships'.

At the 1950 Commercial Motor Show, Saunders displayed its single-deck Rivaloy body mounted on an underfloor-engined Commer Avenger I chassis. This was a 35-seater with full front American-style cab and deep

*Top:* **The last of a batch of 40 Bristol K6As with attractive 56-seat Saunders bodies, delivered to Maidstone & District.** *G.H.F. Atkins*

*Above:* **A small batch of Commer Avenger Is were bodied by Saunders in 1950. This 33-seat example for Mid Wales has the full front and 'American-style' windscreens.**

*Above:* **Saunders won a large export order for 620 bodies on Leyland Royal Tiger chassis for Cuba. This was a two-door 40-seat bus.**

recessed windscreen, the entrance being behind the front axle. It was suitable for home and export markets and could be supplied in completely knocked down or partially knocked down form as required. The body was built in six main units, ie sides, floor, roof, front and rear end and the joining of these components together was extremely simple. This exhibit attracted a great deal of interest, especially from Latin American countries which were eager to expand their transport systems. They could see a particular advantage in the simplicity of assembling the body sections by using their own semi-skilled labour force and the fact that the bodies could be shipped in kit form thus greatly reducing deck space and tariff duty. At about the same time Leyland launched its first underfloor-engined chassis, the Royal Tiger, and its success both at home and abroad was responsible for the virtual collapse in demand for vertical-engined single-deck chassis. It was a combination of the Saunders Rivaloy body and the heavy but strong Royal Tiger chassis that captured a most valuable 10 million dollar order from Cuba for 620 buses, a contract which put both Saunders and the Royal Tiger firmly in the limelight.

At the beginning of 1951 the company changed its name to Saunders-Roe (Anglesey) Ltd and was often better known by the abbreviation of Saro.

The Cuban order for Autobus Modernos of Havana kept the production lines busy between 1950-1953 and encouraged other Latin American companies to look at British-built buses. Argentina ordered 100 Royal Tigers with Saunders bodywork similar to the Havana batch and it was reported that 50 of the Havana buses were redirected to Argentina.

Nearer home an 'export' order was completed for Erne Bus Company of Enniskillen which took delivery of two Royal Tigers with front entrance 44-seat bodywork. They were unusual in the fact that they were the only examples that were 7ft6in wide and had African-style bicycle roof racks. Londonderry and Lough Swilly Railway Co., Londonderry took delivery of four Royal Tigers with centre-entrances in 1951 followed by a further four identical vehicles in 1953.

An interesting 'one off' order in 1951 was for two Rivaloy half-cab bodies mounted on AEC Regal rebuild chassis for Lincolnshire RCC. They had 39-seat rear entrance bodies. Also during 1951 Saunders-Roe introduced the prototype Rivaloy-bodied double-decker. Mounted on an AEC Regent III chassis and seating 56 passengers, the extremely light body weighed only 2tons 3cwt. It underwent an intensive test programme at the MIRA pavè and corrugated track proving ground. Later that year it was painted green and cream and registered OKM 317, then entered service with Maidstone & District as a demonstrator. After demonstration duties it finally entered service with CB Law of Prestwick in 1953 and was then absorbed in the AA (Dodds), Troon fleet the same year, where it has remained ever since; it is now preserved by its owner. During its long service with AA, it has proved to

**The prototype Rivaloy double-deck body was mounted on an AEC Regent III chassis. It was extensively tested at the MIRA test track at Nuneaton, and the rear view (*left*) shows the strong similarities with the Saunders RT bodies. As OKM 317 it was bought by AA, Ayr, (*below*) and is now preserved.** *Saunders-Roe; G. Coxon*

be a very reliable bus and the Saunders body was exceptionally good.

Another small export order was completed in 1952, this time for GNR, Ireland for four Leyland Royal Tigers with 44-seat centre entrance bodywork. This was followed by a substantial export order from Auckland Transport Board, New Zealand. This was for 90 Daimler Freelines, 50 Leyland Royal Tigers, 40 Leyland ETB1 trolleybuses and 12 Bedford SBs. This was part of a modernisation programme which included tram replacement. The bulk of the bodies were shipped in section form. One chassis had three roofs, another three sets of sides and the third three sets of front and rear ends and a box of small parts. On arrival at the dock each chassis was fuelled and driven to the workshops where a special assembly hall had been built to complete the vehicles. The order was later increased to include a further 70 Daimler Freelines and the whole order was shipped between 1951 and 1954.

Back home there was new pressure from operators on both chassis manufacturers and bodybuilders to produce a strong but much lighter vehicle than ever before, partly due to the ever-increasing fuel tax charges, the rule of thumb being for every half-ton saved, half-a-mile a gallon of fuel oil is saved. Leyland had produced the successful Royal Tiger chassis two years previously but this was being criticised for its weight, so Leyland introduced a new lightweight chassis, the Tiger Cub. It was developed in a hurry using established components and mounted in a lightweight frame; few thought it would be a success at the time, but in fact it had a long and successful production span. By this time Leyland had decided to withdraw from the bus bodybuilding market and so Saunders-Roe, having already gained much experience in lightweight bodywork, was approached to body the prototype Tiger Cub. This new lightweight bus was a 44-seater, and the external lines were pleasing to the eye, being well proportioned and practically designed. The body weight turned the scales at 1ton 17cwt and could be further reduced by 4cwt by having a simplified specification. The complete vehicle weighed 5tons

*Above:* **Although Devon General ordered 15 Rivaloy bodies for rebuilt AEC Regal chassis, only one rebuild was bodied by Saunders-Roe, as seen here.** *G.H. Truran*

10cwt, considerably lighter than any previous single-deck underfloor-engined bus. The bus was registered OTC 738 and was used as a demonstrator. This vehicle impressed the BET Federation management, which ordered one for evaluation purposes. It was allocated to the Ribble fleet and appeared at the 1952 Commercial Motor Show. It was the first Tiger Cub to enter service – however, Leyland did make many improvements to the original chassis before it entered service. Also appearing at the 1952 Show was a Rivaloy lightweight-bodied Guy Arab IV double-decker for Birmingham City Transport. It was built to BCT's special requirements, including a straight staircase which limited the seating capacity to 55, and typical Birmingham external mouldings. It was considerably lighter in weight (approx. 15cwt) than other vehicles in its fleet and the intention was to evaluate the new Rivaloy body. However, also appearing at the Show and in direct competition was MCW's lightweight double-deck body, the Orion, which although very spartan became a successful body until the late 1960s.

A large order was placed by the BET Group and between 1953-1954, 148 Saro-bodied Tiger Cubs entered service with the following companies: Ribble (49); East Midland (25); Yorkshire Traction (24); Northern (15); Sunderland District (16); Trent (10); and Thomas Bros (9). It was reported that they proved to be a successful combination and many of these buses remained in service with their original owners until the late 1960s. One of Ribble's Tiger Cubs (412) enjoyed an extended working life with Purple Motors of Bethesda and only recently has it been withdrawn and is now preserved.

Another interesting demonstrator was a Saro-bodied Tiger Cub with a Pneumocyclic gearbox (two-pedal control). It was built by late 1952 and painted in Green Line livery and registered PTE 592. It entered service with London Transport in June 1953 and operated from Dalston and Reigate garages. It was returned to Leyland Motors in April 1954 and after a further period of demonstrations to other operators it was presented to the Leyland Motors Social and Athletic Club in 1958.

In 1953 four more interesting 'one-offs' appeared from the Saunders-Roe bodybuilding works. The first one was on an experimental Guy LUF chassis and had a 44-seat body similar to the ones fitted to the Tiger Cubs. It was registered LJW 336 and was used as a Guy Motors demonstrator until 1955 when it was acquired by Samuel Morgan of Armthorpe. Saunders-Roe was awarded an order from Devon General for 15 lightweight Rivaloy double-deck bodies on AEC Regent chassis (rebuilt from 1938 AEC Regal 1 chassis). The prototype bus was completed in 1953, ETT 995, No 705, and it was the only one built, as Saunders-Roe decided not to make any further vehicles of that type. The remainder of the batch were fitted with lightweight MCW Orion bodywork.

During the previous 2-3 years there had been a mild interest from home-based operators for a lightweight integral single-deck bus. The major manufacturers were combining their resources and as a result Leyland and MCW produced the Olympian and AEC and Park Royal the Monocoach. The main advantages of the integral bus were greater economy of operation and lower initial cost, both of which the operator regarded as important. Saunders-Roe had the experience of producing strong lightweight alloy bodies and so when Maidstone & District came along with an order, the two firms collaborated to produce an integral bus. The specification included such readily-available components as a Gardner 5HLW engine, David Brown 5-speed gearbox and an Eaton 2-speed rear axle.

*Above:* **Two Saro bodies for Auckland, New Zealand – a Daimler Freeline and a Bedford SB.**

The body style was similar to the Saro-Tiger Cubs, except that the emergency exit was towards the rear of the offside, thus complying with the draft provisions of the revised Conditions of Fitness Regulations. It was numbered 5068, RKE 540 and had 43 seats. It remained unique, as no further integrals were built.

The last 'one-off' was the Saunders-Roe-bodied prototype low-loader rear engined double-decker. This was a completely new design of chassis from Leyland, and Saunders-Roe produced a modern and well-proportioned body which incorporated a full front and an open rear platform. It had a total seating capacity of 61, 37 upstairs and 24 downstairs. It was registered STF 90 and after some initial testing appeared at the 1954 Commercial Motor Show. After a further period of demonstration around the country it was sold to Lowland Motorways of Glasgow in 1957.

1954 was to be the final year of producing bus bodies. The last order to be completed was for Liverpool City Transport, which took two AEC Regent IIIs with 58-seat rear entrance bodywork. They were delivered in November 1954 and were reported to be two of the best bodies the department had ever purchased.

During Saunders-Roe's nine years production it can be seen that some very interesting buses were produced. It was market leader in producing very light and strong alloy bodywork. It also succeeded in winning some large important export contracts, utilising the concept of producing bodywork in sections, thus reducing shipping charges and enabling local semi-skilled labour to complete their own vehicles. It can be seen from its history that Saunders-Roe did not receive many repeat orders and apart from the London Transport and BET Group orders most of the other orders were small in quantity. The competition in the bodybuilding industry was extremely competitive by the early 1950s and it was inevitable that some of the competitors would have to drop out; unfortunately Saunders-Roe was one.

Overall Saunders-Roe produced approximately 1800 bus bodies and of these approximately two-thirds went for export – a great achievement.

# North Western Frontiers

**When the North Western Road Car Co was dismembered in 1972, its buses passed into the hands of Crosville, Selnec, Trent and National Travel. Photographs by R.L. WILSON**

Two of North Western's once-numerous fleet of BET-style single-deck vehicles in different hands after the split-up. LDB 769 (*Above*) was a 1959 Leyland Tiger Cub PSUC1/2 with Willowbrook bodywork, seen in 1973 in Crosville ownership. RDB 871, an AEC Reliance/Willowbrook of 1961, passed to Selnec (Cheshire) and is seen at Altrincham (*below*) in 1972, in North Western red with Selnec lettering.

*Above:* **In 1962 North Western took 10 of these Leyland Leopards with multi-windowed 11metre Alexander bodies. When seen in 1972 it was operating on hire to North Western Coachways.**

*Below:* **The Alexander Y-type body replaced the version shown above in 1962, and this North Western Leopard of 1963 passed to Trent. It is seen in Buxton in 1972.**

*Above:* **In pre-NBC Trent livery at Stockport in 1972, an ex-North Western AEC Reliance with 53-seat Willowbrook bodywork.**

*Below:* **At Macclesfield in 1973 on loan to Crosville, another ex-North Western Reliance/Willowbrook in the Trent fleet in standard NBC livery.**

*Above:* **North Western bought 40 of these Bristol RESL6G with Marshall bodies in 1968, which ended up split between Selnec and Crosville. In the fleet of Greater Manchester, Selnec's successor, 286 is seen in 1975.**

*Below:* **In all-over Crosville green, the former North Western 308 at Bangor in 1980. On withdrawal in 1981 it became a Crosville service vehicle.**

*Above:* **The big North Western fleet of AEC Renowns with Park Royal bodywork was split between Crosville and Selnec. This 1963 example is seen with Crosville at Northwich shortly after acquisition in 1972.**

*Below:* **One of the 1964 batch of Renowns in the Selnec (Southern) fleet in Portland Street, Manchester, in 1973. It was withdrawn in 1977.**

*Above:* **North Western also went for the Dennis Loline between 1960 and 1962. This was the first of these buses, with East Lancs body, in Selnec (Cheshire) ownership in 1972.**

*Below:* **The 1962 batch were Loline III with Alexander bodies, and the former North Western 903 is seen at Macclesfield in 1974, after passing to Crosville.**

*Above:* **North Western bought 85 Alexander-bodied Daimler Fleetlines between 1963 and 1967 – its last double-deckers. No. 188 from the 1965 batch was one of the first North Western buses to appear in full Selnec livery, only a month after the take-over. This was one of two Fleetlines delivered with experimental Compas heating, hence the shorter lower deck window and extra grilles.**

*Right:* **One of the 1967 batch after transfer to Crosville, approaching Wilmslow in April 1972.**

*Facing page:* **The Golden age of the mini dress, 1: Basle, a slim little girl and a slim little tram.**

# Skirt

**ROBERT E. JOWITT makes some interesting comparisons**

If your studies and researches or your pursuits of simple idle pleasure should happen to take you into the realms of Victorian fashion plates you will encounter, during the 1870s and 1880s, skirts with a curious protuberance about the hinder quarters known as a *bustle*. If, on the other hand, your studies and researches or your pursuits of simple idle pleasure should happen to take you into the realms of buses, you will encounter, not quite a century later, Fleetlines and Atlanteans with a curious protuberance at the rear known as . . . yes, a *bustle*!

Connoisseurs of fashions and of buses might be forgiven for considering the bustle an unbeautiful feature. It has been suggested that the garment

would be more suitable for a giraffe, as there is room for four legs within its copious tenting. As for the back of the bus, various attempts have been made to disguise the bulge but it never entirely disappeared, and to this day bustles on the backs of buses in Oporto provide a free if hot and illegal and precarious seat for the local urchins, like the bufferbeams of the trams for an earlier generation.

In the generation of bustles on ladies, and indeed for several generations afterwards, the skirts, with or without bustles, swept the ground so that the glimpse of a lady's ankle was enormously exciting. But to see it, you had to wait for a very windy day or a lady in a hurry at a crossing hitching up her skirt a bit higher than she might have done normally, in her haste to flee from the oncoming omnibus horses of the LGOC.

Despite the depth of hemline, public transport authorities went to some pains to fit *decency boards* on the upper decks of their tramcars and omnibuses, in order that ladies travelling thereon should not risk passers-by catching a sight of their ankles.

In Britain, that was. Not so in Paris, where the vast and varied range of monstrous double-deckers – horse trams, compressed-air trams, accumulator trams, steam trams, contact-stud trams, overhead electric trams, horse omnibuses and even primitive autobuses – yes, all these had but the scantiest protection on the upper deck, hardly enough to prevent you from falling out, let alone prevent the boys on the pavement giving your button boots the eye.

But Paris of course was always a wicked city.

Anyway, whether or not decency boards were a necessity when they were introduced, fashion in the course of time would have rendered them unnecessary even if bus design had not advanced to the point where what had once been special boards were now just part of the bus flanks. From the turn of the century, ladies' hemlines crawled slowly upwards until by the Charleston era it was possible to see *knees*. A popular verse of the 1920s sums up the matter thus:

*Half an inch, half an inch, half an inch shorter*
*Skirts are the same for both mother and daughter*
*When the winds blow*
*Both of them show*
*Half an inch, half an inch more than they oughter.*

So far as bus fashions were concerned, on the other hand, the hemline was by now starting to droop. At least in Britain.

Consider London, the B type, the K type, the NS, the LT; the skirt was growing lower and lower. But in Paris the hemline stayed up all through the 1920s and 1930s, the last series of prewar buses, the Renaults of 1936-8, showed almost as much of the

*Left:* **Full skirts of the late 1950s plus Chausson of the early 1950s bouncing over the cobblestones in Lille (or possibly Tourcoing or Roubaix, or somewhere in the Nord of France).**

*Above:* **Tight skirts in the early 1960s. Just above the knee. The inspector on the Ghent tramways, Belgium, keeps his attention on his duties rather than the enticing spectacle of the girl scratching her calf.**

underside as the Schneiders of before the previous war. This is odd when one remembers that Paris is the centre of the fashion world and that ladies' hemlines during the 1930s were imitating the London bus and drooping rapidly.

Meanwhile in Berlin hemlines of buses were (give or take a few oddments) following British trends. Other German tendencies at this time were set to produce world wide disaster. World War 2 brought about all manner of curious and hideous fashions, British bus examples being the utility vehicles all square at the corners and with uncomfortable wooden seats (not that the latter affected the outside appearance), while ladies' fashions were in general equally utilitarian and angular, the spirit of them summed up by the *snood*. An ugly name for an ugly thing. If you want to find out more about the snood study contemporary fashion accounts, and you will surely conclude that the snood was quite as bizarre as the utility bus.

Even when the war was over a sad state of affairs continued for several years, until rationing was withdrawn. The end of clothes coupons may be regarded as the beginning of a trend, little marked at first, for fashions to plunge into most unpredictable directions. The end of petrol rationing started a trend, equally little noticed at first, for everyone to be a car owner; which trend was bound in the end to have a bad effect on the fleets of buses, still-extant-prewar and utility and postwar-but-traditional, which were transporting the girls who were now starting to wear skirts which swirled widely and flourishingly somewhere just above mid-calf. So the bus designers had to modernise their ideas. While girls' hemlines started to work upwards bus hemlines remained at the same depth, but on single-deckers the engine retreated under the floor. The result was full-fronted buses, and this on occasion produced a smart decorative feature: a chrome strip or band at headlight level, as for example on various Saro and Weymann Tiger Cubs. This feature could be compared to the wide gold or silver (actually plastic) belts worn by teenage nymphs to support their multiple stiff petticoats and flared-out knee-revealing skirts while dancing, pony-tails tossing, to Bill Haley and Elvis Presley.

Alternative wear for bopping was very tight jeans and very floppy sweaters, and if single-decks were tucking their engines out of sight double-decks were having a last fling with the traditional front engine, exemplified by AEC Renowns as neat and prettily curved as tight blue jeans. But here and there rear-engine double-deckers began to infiltrate, revolutionary in appearance, bustle at the back.

This did not cause girls to revert to bustles. No, skirts continued upwards. There was a post-Haley-era pop song – you could hear it relayed on fairground loud-speakers as jungle rides and dodgems circled crazily and, half hidden behind the booths and stalls, you could see prewar half-cab buses, Dennis Lancets and similar delights, pushed off the road by the new generation and serving to transport hooplas and swing-boats – and this song described the merits of 'girls, girls, with their short short skirts, just above the knee'. And on the dodgems and jungle rides were the girls themselves. Skirts just above the knee, and very tight round the thighs, so the girls could hardly move their legs except from the knees down, and had an awful struggle to climb the steep steps of the underfloor-engine buses which carried them home from the fairgrounds to their parents awaiting them with complaints about the brevity of their skirts.

But if memory does not play us false there came, before the 1960s started swinging, a period when the just-above-the-knee skirt acquired respectability, coinciding with the period when Atlanteans and suchlike bustled (oh, dear!) in ever increasing numbers about the streets of several British cities. The streets of London, however, remained populated by thoroughly conservative RMs and RTs, and those of Paris by equally conservative Chaussons and Somuas and even more conservative prewar veterans. As for what was happening in Berlin at this moment, we have to admit to being not very sure, but Berlin by now didn't really count any more, Bonn had become the Federal capital. Bonn

*Left:* **Trousers with loops underfoot were much favoured by German girls, but are seen here (on numbers 2, 3 and 4 from the left) on lasses in Blackpool. The round baskets were a very English fashion. The tram style was entirely Blackpool.**

*Below:* **A chic Parisienne could make even a trouser suit look attractive. The Paris buses of the 1930s still looked good in their short skirts 35 years later.**

had a fleet of postwar trams and trolleybuses as boring and stodgily Germanic as the Sunday suits of middle aged *Hausfrauen*. The girls in Bonn, and also in fact in Cologne and Dortmund and lots of other German cities, were in large measure very very beautiful, even if their hems always seemed lower than English ones; but some of them indulged in a dreadful fashion of trousers which were stretched to shapeless tubes by means of a loop under the foot, the latter being usually shod in clattering Dr Scholl sandal, the ensemble as floppy and unalluring as an articulated *Grossraumwagen*. Another curious fashion at this time was the hipster, which in jeans form produced excruciatingly flared legs and in skirt form kept the hem where it had been before and in both forms lowered the waist to somewhere down round the hips. The mode was much adopted, along with stripey shirts, by a faction known as the *Mods*. It could be argued that the hipsters were derived from the chrome bands on the early underfloor engine buses, but the fashion was certainly never reflected in subsequent bus design. Bus fashion at this date actually went back in time, with some very smart Bristol coaches with the rear windows of the saloon higher above the waist than the front windows, imitating a vogue of three decades earlier. Stylish as it was, it cannot have been favourably regarded, for the vehicles, replaced by MWs with straight waists, were soon to be found operating in roles much more humble than the luxury trips for which they were intended.

But is this surprising? The 1960s were starting to swing, in music and morals and fashions – fashions both female and bus. Paris began to invest in a fleet of underfloor-engine bulbous-windscreen Saviems and Berliets which if quite horribly untraditional were to prove remarkably successful and in their later years to attain (as nearly as a bus can) a petit

*Left:* **The Golden Age of the mini dress, 2: London, pursuit of RM.**

*Below:* **The Golden Age of the mini dress, 3: Bournemouth, exquisite legs and a nice trolleybus too.**

bourgeois complacency. London embarked on a series of adventures quite as disgustingly modernistic as their French counterpart but mostly far less suitable for their purposes. And girls' fashions reached their most glorious height above the ground. If, in certain instances, the mini skirt was as unsuitable on various shapes of girl (short and fat) as the DMS was unsuitable for various routes in London, on a great number of girls the mini skirt was one of the most perfect fashions ever.

Curiously staid in this outrageous period were several batches of Bristol REs, not very swinging, less bold than the coaches of a few years earlier, but handsome all the same. Was it felt that if girls were to dress so skimpily and other buses were to be so flightily florid, Bristols should stick smartly to sensible taste?

Alas, the golden age could not last, and the mini skirts and the mini dresses and the neat if not highly fashionable mini suits began to give way. And the REs too. The most obvious rival to the mini skirt was the maxi skirt – or was it called the midi skirt? – which like a sermon was long and boring. Flared jeans, derived from the mods of the early 1960s, were much in evidence, and the trouser suit, a derivation of flared jeans, made some sorties out from the seedy saloon bars where it really seemed most at home into the pages of high class magazines. Skirts and dresses went ethnic and flapped even more than flared jeans, and flared jeans went out of the window, to be replaced by thoroughly dreadful boiler suits and parachute suits. Buses, during all this anarchy, became by contrast decidedly dull, being nearly all Bristol VRs which didn't keep up the standards of the REs, or Leyland Nationals which some people find as unpleasing to look at as boiler suits.

Yet while boiler suits became ever more baggy

**After the mini era you couldn't for some time tell where hemlines would go, but by 1980 they seemed to have settled below the knee. Crinkly curls were much in vogue too. In the background is a West Midlands Fleetline with a bustle.**

**Golden Age of tightly stretched jeans and Leyland Nationals, these examples being in Alfreton.**

and bloated there suddenly shone forth in the last couple of years a ray of light, girls decided they wanted to look shapely and feminine again, or shapely anyway, and emerged in jeans even tighter than the tight jeans of the 1960s; and then feminine too, for, wonder of wonders, the mini skirt returned. Not quite with the same trim brevity of the golden age, slightly more carefree and casual, but definitely mini.

We have to wonder whether this wonderful revival will last. We can only hope so. But can we hope for a revival of the bus fashions which were the current mode in the original mini skirt high noon? It seems as unlikely as a revival of bustles on girls. The heavenly vision of tiny mini on RT staircase is gone for ever.

In conclusion, we must apologise for the fact that space does not permit for a discussion on the fashions of so-called 'topless' buses. Or girls.

# Taken Over: 2

*Above:* **An unusual machine for Midland Red, a Northern Counties-bodied Leyland Titan PD3A/1 acquired with the business of Harper Bros, Heath Hayes in 1974.** *G.R. Mills*

*Below:* **South Yorkshire PTE has systematically acquired many of the independent bus operators in its area. Many of the buses taken over have had this style of Roe bodywork; this Daimler Fleetline CRG6LX came from the Blue Ensign fleet in 1978.** *G.R. Mills*

*Above:* **In 1974 Cleveland Transit acquired the independent Saltburn Motor Services, along with several vehicles including this 1970 Bedford VAM70 with 48-seat Plaxton body.** *G.R. Mills*

*Below:* **United took several non-standard buses into stock in the 1960s and 1970s following acquisition of local independents. This AEC Reliance with Plaxton 55-seat bodywork came with the fleet of Wilkinson's Motor Services, Sedgefield, in 1967.** *G.R. Mills*

# What a Water Bus!

DAVID KAYE

If you stood for a while in the centre of Lincoln today it might not be long before Lincoln City Transport's No 43 (KTL 43 Y) passed before your eyes – a smart Leyland Olympian in cream and Lincoln green livery. However, back in June 1982 spectators alongside Brayford Pool watching the annual Lincoln Water Festival caught a glimpse of an earlier No 43, also in cream and Lincoln green, but of somewhat different appearance and mode of propulsion. For LCT 1 X was the Transport Department entry in the fancy floats race, competing with the Royal Barge (including Lincoln Imp seated aloft) and an appropriate entry by the local hospital's X-rays Department. Genuine seats from a former bus had been fixed to both decks, whilst a sweating crew of Department employees sat in the lower saloon armed with oars. The Saturday turned out to be excessively hot and the crew found that 'driving' their vehicle for one and a half circuits of this large lake took a great deal out of them, and, regretfully, I have to report that they came in last of the trio.

In June 1979 there appeared equally briefly on the Lincolnshire scene an equally bizarre 'bus'. The Horncastle Bus Club, as part of its money raising activities that summer, decided to stage a Country Craft Fayre at the village of Scamblesby, mid-way between the Louth and Horncastle terminii of their route. As part of the afternoon's festivities a local drama group performed an improvised play taking the mickey out of the Club in the gentlest and kindest fashion. Their skit involved a diversion of the route via the hamlet of Claxby Pluckacre (which does really exist in the Wolds). The snag was that a dragon inhabited a cave there and would not let the bus pass through its territory. The bus in question was represented by a hardboard cut-out, looking rather like an early Ford Model 'T' single-decker, and propelled by semi-hidden members of the cast, who carried it across the playground 'stage' upon cue. Like the water bus mentioned above both performers and spectators willingly joined in the fantasy. After all, although many plays and films have trains featuring in them, few use buses, yet probably a larger percentage of the population use the latter than the former mode of transport each year.

My third and final Lincolnshire vignette involving the entertainment value of the bus comes from the 1982 Tulip Parade in Spalding, when before the first military band or float hove into sight along the procession route through that town, cheers greeted an old open topper used by Michelin Tyres for advertising purposes, and on the upper deck of which a jazz band played the inevitable 'When the Saints Come Marching Home'. Since black clouds were lowering over the area, a cool breeze had arisen, and the first spots of rain fell, this apparition stiffened the resolve of the faint-hearted to stick it out until the main procession arrived to its usual accompaniment of 'ooo's' and 'ahs' from the huge crowds.

Yes, the bus does have a role other than transporting genuine passengers from Jerusalem to Skellingthorpe, from Pode Hole to Cuckoo Bridge, and from Tumby Woodside to New York.

# What you Can (and Can't) do with PASS CAMBRIA

**Another good reason to visit mid-Wales. By A. MOYES**

*Pass Cambria* was introduced in April 1983 as an unlimited travel ticket on public transport in mid-Wales, by Mid Wales Development. This agency, like the Highlands and Islands Development Board, undertakes a wide range of strategies to improve the economy of the area for which it has a remit; in its case it operates in the county of Powys and the districts of Ceredigion and Meirionydd. Since at least two of its officers were formerly on the staff of HIDB and were responsible for devising the Highlands and Islands Travelpass, there are not surprisingly similarities between the two pass packages. Notably, both agencies have published comprehensive area timetables which present a tempting set of opportunities for journey-making. Secondly, both area passes conveniently extend their coverage to allow pass-holders to begin and end their journeys some way outside the area for which these agencies are responsible. Thirdly, the validity of both passes is not absolutely unlimited. In *Pass Cambria*'s case, it can be used on nine bus operators' services. But a further eighteen independents' services appear in the Mid Wales Travel Planner on which *Pass Cambria* is not at present accepted. Admittedly these are almost wholly services operating on the very edge of the mid-Wales area, and in many cases are very sparse. This contribution will try to indicate some of the things that the *Pass Cambria* holder can (and cannot) do and see, of public transport interest. No time-scale is suggested for a visit, but both one- and two-week versions are available, and unlike the Highlands pass there is no seasonal surcharge. The £1 Travel Planner is, additionally, free to *Pass Cambria* buyers.

It must be said that British Rail has some advantages for access to parts of mid-Wales. Aged diesel multiple units provide up to half a dozen weekday trips each way on the Shrewsbury-Aberystwyth and -Swansea, Cambrian Coast, and Blaenau Ffestiniog branches. It would be difficult, dogmatic and unwise utterly to avoid them. The loyal coach fan would however be drawn to two regular facilities: the Cheltenham-to-Aberystwyth 640, and the pair of Traws

**Pulling out of Capel Trisant on a Monday trip from Devils Bridge to Aberystwyth in September 1983, an ex-Whittle Bedford/Duple. Since August 1982 the service has been operated by J.A. Evans, Tregaron, instead of Crosville.**
*All photos: A. Moyes*

Cambria services from Cardiff to north Wales (700/1). These have quite different origins and character.

The 640 formed part of the famous Cheltenham interchange and, like many of the services connecting there, was initiated by Black & White Motorways, in its case in 1930. Almost unchanged for half a century, it plied daily and somewhat leisurely via Hereford, Leominster (refreshment stop), then west along the A44 for another three hours, apart from diving off to serve Llandrindod Wells. Placed into National Travel (West) in 1973, and then transferred to South Wales Transport operation in May 1981, it kept the standard features of pre-booking and lodging turns for the drivers. Although filling a large, otherwise empty space on the National Express map, and offering a valuable interurban facility for the towns en route, 640 suffered from thinnish midweek and winter traffic. It was not helped by development from 1974 of an alternative daily service out of Aberystwyth, the 670, to Carmarthen, south Wales and the Severn Bridge, giving faster times to London via the M4, and cheaper fares than via Cheltenham. A July 1981 change was to reroute 640 between Cheltenham and Leominster to serve Malvern and Worcester, in theory providing a local bus through the rustic delights of Hanley Swan also. Fourteen months later, Crosville took over the 640, cutting days of operation to Fridays and Saturdays only, though it has gradually been restored to daily running in summer 1983. It has been speeded up, to allow out-and-back operation by Aberystwyth drivers, and one of the local Leyland Leopard/ Duple coaches (ELL 508) was duly repainted in National white for it. In practice, as likely a contender would be one of Crosville's several ex-Ribble ECW-bodied Bristol RELH6L coaches which have settled well in this new home. *Pass Cambria* is valid for journeys between Cheltenham and points including and west of Kington.

The Traws Cambria express services, in contrast, cater for movement between south and north Wales. In their present form they are quite young, although Crosville and Western Welsh began a joint Cardiff-mid Wales-Liverpool route in 1964. The senior of the two present services is the 700, from Cardiff via Merthyr, Brecon, Llandrindod Wells, Newtown, Machynlleth, Porthmadog and Caernarfon, to Bangor. It began in June 1979 under prompting by the Welsh Office, with a journey each way four days per week. It was augmented to daily during subsequent summers. Service 701 began in May 1980. In winters it offers a return journey on the same four days per week (Friday to Monday) from Cardiff to Swansea, Carmarthen, Aberystwyth and Machynlleth, where it connects with 700. In summer it continues in tandem with 700 for a while, then travels on via Blaenau Ffestiniog and Llandudno to Rhyl on these four days, increasing to daily south of Machynlleth. A daily return working from Aberystwyth to Cardiff is now also labelled 701; this is most of the old National Travel 670 referred to earlier. The May 1980 upgrading also featured a route 702 which originally ran daily, between Cardiff, Newport, Newtown and Liverpool. It was a descendent of the Crosville-Western Welsh 1964 innovation also mentioned earlier, but despite this pedigree it ceased in January 1981. In practice, its northern half is covered by some of Crosville's 'Townlynx' expresses, and the southern part by Cross Gates Motors' Llandrindod Wells – Cardiff express, on both of which the *Pass* is accepted. Although Crosville and National Welsh began Traws Cambria mainly with Leyland Leopard/Duple coaches, both had dedicated newer coaches to the services in 1983. Crosville uses Willowbrook-bodied Leopards, and National Welsh has a trio of its Plaxton Paramount-bodied Leyland Tigers in a special green-and-red striped livery. At times of stress, the mixed blessing of older stock may appear; on the Machynlleth-Aberystwyth section of 701, for instance, a Bristol VRT dd may provide cover between Tuesday and Thursday to allow a National Welsh vehicle to work out and back from Cardiff in the same day. The Traws Cambria services deliberately allow connections with local bus services and British Rail.

Long distance Crosville bus trips within the mid Wales area are becoming easier too because of the linking of long-established, infrequent inter-town services, with local authority support. The essentially rail-replacement service between Wrexham and Barmouth dates from 1964; the Shrewsbury-Newtown-Llanidloes link came six years later. Through services between Aberystwyth and Dolgellau, and

Aberystwyth and Carmarthen were forged in 1976, and in August 1982 a marathon route S52 was created which in one case allows travel on the same vehicle from north of Machynlleth through Aberystwyth and Ammanford to Swansea. South Wales Transport took a small stake in this route in June 1983. Scenically all of these routes are well worth the ride; the only quibble might be the fairly high probability of travel in a B series Leyland National bus, although Crosville is by no means without dual purpose A series versions. One of these, re-engined with Gardner power, is presently operated from Dolgellau, fleet number ENG 867; vehicles in this part of Crosville's empire are subject to frequent overnight shifts in allocation, however, partly because of the development of these long routes. Other NBC subsidiaries do enter the *Pass Cambria* area's southern edge, namely South Wales Transport at Brecon, meeting National Welsh there. The latter's appearances, bound for Cardiff and Abergavenny, are also relevant for pass holders. SWT will almost invariably produce Leyland Nationals on its Swansea-Brecon service, National Welsh anything from dual-purpose Nationals to downgraded Leopard or Bristol RELH coaches, to RESL buses, on inter-town routes that give impressive views of the Black Mountains.

Of Crosville's subordinate routes in the *Pass Cambria* area, it is difficult to provide a full gourmet's guide, especially since some gourmets have highly selective palates. A personal favourite would be the Pontrhydfendigaid circular service from Aberystwyth three times per day, which deserves at least four stars: six, if it were one of the Monday variants that serves Cnwch Coch. The routes (for almost every timing is slightly different) treat one to glimpses of a stately home, lead mine remains, bleak emptinesses of moorland, lush wooded valleys broad and narrow, and some very tight lanes. The circulars combine a very long-established Crosville route (initiated in 1925) with bits of others picked up in the 1970s following abandonment by Lloyd Jones, Pontrhydygroes. Further north, at Bala, Crosville's Thursday market locals may still produce the company's last surviving Bristol RESL buses, and at school times, ex-Southdown Bristol VRT dds on publicly-timetabled school trips from the Corwen area. The Uwchaled community minibus may also be seen there, on the noon departure from native Cerrigydruidion, and 1500hrs return, though this and its other activities are conspicuously absent from the Travel Planner. Moving a little east, the Welshpool town service to Bryn Sirol has a little character in its early stages, and could feature Bristol RELL buses. Those of an economical turn of mind will appreciate that the fastest way of "saving" money for pass holders is by making large numbers of short, relatively expensive journeys.

The only other large non-independent operator in the *Pass Cambria* area is the Post Office, with a dozen vehicles in the area, allocated to nine routes. These are perhaps best explored on afternoon trips. As part of the pioneer (1967) service at Llanidloes, for instance, there's an engaging foray to Llidiartywaun and Tylwch to round off the day's work. Ten years elapsed before more routes were set up in Wales. The standard Dodge postbus has re-established public transport to some spots served only fitfully by orthodox services in years gone by, such as Tirabad, Abbeycwmhir and Blaenpennal, and to others like Abergwesyn and Dylife that were probably never reached by bus previously. The Machynlleth service employs a Talbot Avenger estate car and covers a contorted web of lanes on its morning sortie that defies mapping and takes six hours. The afternoon Aberystwyth to Blaenpennal trip is perhaps the most convenient to sample, though note that it starts from the rear of the Post Office in Chalybeate Street behind "No Admittance" signs.

Taking NBC, PO and independents together, Aberystwyth counts as the richest bus centre in the *Pass Cambria* area, with nine operators serving it. In descending order of richness are Lampeter (8), Newtown (7), Builth and Llandrindod Wells (6 each), Aberaeron and Brecon (5 each), Newcastle Emlyn, Cardigan and Llandyssul (4 each), Machynlleth, Tregaron, Welshpool and Llanfyllin (3 each), Dolgellau (2) and Bala (1). This richness may be more apparent than real, since a town need only to be on the Traws Cambria network to be credited with two operators. Few of the independents have networks of any size or frequency, and sightings of their activities may involve careful planning. Meirionydd district offers the least to the independent-hunter – a solitary

minibus service at Harlech.
Ceredigion is another matter; four independents' services are pass-eligible, and are a varied bunch. David Evans, Penrhyncoch, runs modern Bedford coaches out to his home village from Aberystwyth, and Ford Transits and Austin Ambassador taxis on feeder trips, most of which could, in today's jargon, be described as demand-responsive. Also in Aberystwyth appears David James, Llangeitho, again with Bedford coaches including a fairly late model narrow SB, but two nippy Bristol LHS/Plaxton coaches are also owned. James' climax is at Lampeter on Tuesdays, with up to five vehicles present. Having taken over some Crosville routes into Aberaeron in 1982, he is also more evident there on the harbourside at that attractive small town. Lampeter can also produce Gwalia's generally oldish coaches bound for Newcastle Emlyn, D. D. Davies'; ageing Ford Transit making indirectly for Llandyssul, Davies' (Pencader) Bedford/Duple buses on the trunk service to Carmarthen, and on Tuesdays perhaps Thomas, Llangadock's, Marshall-bodied Leyland Tiger Cub bus. Most independents' vehicles lay over on the yard by the secondary school.

Still in Ceredigion, three relative newcomers to stage work should be noted at Aberystwyth; J. Alwyn Evans of Tregaron has gradually taken over several Crosville school contracts and related services and permits, to Devils Bridge for example, on which Bedford coaches of varied vintage appear. Emrys Roberts took over some other Crosville timings along the A44 road eastwards in August 1982, which can produce a modernistically-liveried ex-Trimdon Leyland Leopard/Willowbrook bus with meticulous destination blinds. And finally, A R Lewis, Llanrhystud, has some peak-hour timings on the Aberystwyth to Aberaeron road on which an ex-Delaine Bedford/Duple coach is usually provided. None of these three presently accept *Pass Cambria*, nor do the trio of independents working into Cardigan (Richards, Midway and Daniels). The first two have vehicular

**An ageing and since-withdrawn Gwalia Bus Service Bedford SB/Plaxton leaves Pontsian bound for Lampeter from Newcastle Emlyn in 1978 – a Pass Cambria-valid route.**

appeal in the form of smart ex-Maidstone Bedford/Duple buses, and ex-City of Oxford Ford/Willowbrook buses respectively.

In Powys, the independents are thinly spread and not too easy to patronise, even though some of the routes are well worth sampling. Other than on the main NBC-covered axes in Montgomery and Brecon districts, the picture is essentially of once-or twice-weekly services on some but not all of the main 'A' roads, a slowly increasing number of school contracts available to the public, and little else. However when the county of Powys was formed in 1974, contract services were provided for transferred employees of the old constituent counties to the new county hall at Llandrindod Wells. Some of these were eventually made public, along with newer contracts to the county's Further Education college completed in Newtown in 1980. So some links have gained or regained coverage on five or six days per week, even if the identity of the contractor has changed from time to time.

The Powys independents are a mixture of old- and new-established businesses, dependent largely on obtaining – and holding onto – school contracts. Mid Wales Motorways in the 1950s could boast a wonderfully-varied fleet of more than 50 vehicles; now it has about a dozen. Competition from the much-expanded Price of Montgomery led in September 1981 to the latter's school contracts being publicly licensed, often running a few minutes before Mid Wales's stage services, especially on the Newtown-Montgomery-Welshpool route. Not surprisingly, these were virtually abandoned in January 1983. Mid Wales Motorways retains a handful of publicly-available contracts and what are now among the few independent stage services on unclassified roads in the county; that to Mochdre is recommended. Price's nucleus was the Bradley & Lane business across the border at Clun. Hence one Trefaldwyn offering at Newtown bus station on Tuesdays may be a new three-and-two seating Duple-bodied Bedford bus, having swung in over the hills past timing points as exotic as 'Anchor' and

**A morning Aberystwyth-Pontrhydfendigaid circular returns to town through Llanfihangel-y-Creuddyn. Pass Cambria holders could thereby have sampled Crosville B series National SNL 591; until 1970 Lloyd Jones, Pontrhydygroes covered this section.**

PASS CAMBRIA

**Almost Pass Cambria-eligible – Crosville Bristol FS6G DFG234 was at Aberystwyth as a trainer in April 1983 when a vehicle shortage led to it being used on the Llandre School contract. It was photographed on this duty near Capel Dewi on the afternoon of 20 April, 1983.**

'Block'. Newtown bus station that day will also host Owen of Knighton, Roy Brown of Builth Wells, and Cross Gates Motors of Llandrindod Wells, as well as Crosville. All the independent extras have come in on main roads from their respective bases, though that does not rob their routes of scenic quality.

The last two named businesses lead thought naturally into the bus scene in Radnor district, which in some respects is more interesting for its past than present. For a small remote town in thinly-populated country, Llandrindod Wells seems to have exercised an irrational fascination for operators based elsewhere. Perhaps they envisaged busy summer traffic in a Victorian spa which was by inter-war losing its sparkle. Crosville started to build up a four-vehicle system in 1924, quite disconnected from its other operations, and graduating to premises in grandiosely named Oxford Street in 1928. Despite poor viability, up to five trips were built up per weekday thence to Rhayader and Builth Wells, and less frequently to Kington. The company's presence was emphasised by its spattering standard cast-iron bus stop signs around, of which some survive in Greater Llandrindod. In early postwar years, R T Knill (Cross Gates Motors) began to develop from a garage appropriately at Cross Gates by acquiring a thin service to Newtown, then in January 1952 taking over Crosville's Kington service. Three months later the Llandrindod Wells services of Yeomans Motors were brought into the fold. Through a subsidiary, Radnorshire Motors, Yeomans had been so bold as to run every two hours from Llandrindod to Ludlow, evolve an express service to Cardiff, run market-day fill-ins at Knighton, and pioneer entrancing Saturday services into the fastness of Abbeycwmhir and beyond. In 1956, Knill took over the remaining Crosville Radnor operations, added most of Sargeant's services in the Newbridge/Rhayader area in 1962, and mopped up the coach firm of Pritchard, Llandrindod in 1980. Cross Gates has thus been in a good position to respond to the rebirth of the town's hotel trade, especially in relation to SAGA holidays. Apart from the County Hall services, the remaining stage operations are now very thin, the Knighton service and those to Abbeycwmhir having evaporated in the 1960s; the survivors will usually yield modern, mostly first-hand Bedford-Duple coaches.

Sargeant, Builth, survives as a minibus operator with one solitary route, a Monday offering into utterly gulch country to Rhulen. This is not far from the birthplace of Roy Brown's coaches, at oddly-named Hundred House, a non-place five miles out towards Kington. As D. J. Brown, this business could at one time boast some quite audacious market routes such as a direct marathon over the mountains through Glascwm to Hereford; it also ran a short-lived daily rail replacement service to Brecon. Essentially what is left is Monday operation to Llanwrtyd Wells (which once was run by Sargeant every weekday, and even reached Llandovery on Fridays), and a long main road service to Hereford four days per week (passes not accepted, unfortunately) which thanks to NBC's disappearance in the Hay-on-Wye area can now be more effective there. Thinner services to Brecon, Newtown and Aberystwyth complete the picture, the latter two being only newly-

*Above:* **One of the three National Welsh Leyland Tiger/Plaxton Paramount 3200 coaches which carry Traws Cambria livery. No. UC1198 romps through Commins Coch near Aberystwyth on a Rhyl-Cardiff timing on 29 August, 1983.**

*Left:* **Characteristically standing on the Park Avenue car park by the railway station, two vehicles from the fleet of Roberts, Aberystwyth – ex- Ladvale AEC Reliance/ Plaxton and ex-Trimdon Leyland Leopard/ Willowbrook, both labelled for the ex-Crosville service to Cwmrheidol in April 1983.**

PASS CAMBRIA

**New variety in the James, Llangeitho fleet: a Duple-bodied Leyland Leopard at the town hall, Lampeter, bound for home on a Tuesday-only timing in August 1983, which Pass Cambria holders could freely use.**

*Right:* **The author's first 'steer' – the ex-Hebble Albion Valkyrie PW67 with Brush body, new in 1933 as JX 1407, in the yard of Norfolk's at Nayland in 1953.** *All photos: G.R. Mills*

developed. To round off the independents of the area one should record the cluster of pass-eligible services run by Williams, Cwmdu which were inherited from Charles Davies, Talgarth, in 1974. Only the Brecon-Talgarth route through Llangorse with its attractive lake operates with any frequency; it will treat you to one or other of the company's 24 Bedford/Duple coaches. The centre of operations is now at Rich Way, Brecon, not far from the National Welsh depot. At Brecon, too, T. R. Williams' minibus loop northwards around Merthyr Cynog is the sole survivor of a web of mainly Friday routes which once touched Llaneglwys, Llanfihangel-nant-Bran, Heol Senni and other now implausible destinations.

These, then, represent something of the psv endowment of mid Wales and its potential for the *Pass Cambria* holder. As a marketing exercise, Mid Wales Development promoted a Festival of Transport in June 1983 at which the *Pass* was officially launched. This included such attractions as an open top dd of Crosville operating along the seafront, numerous cross-country links over quite unprecedented roads, using minibuses and preserved buses, extra trains, pleasure boats and even horse-drawn vehicles. The Festival is likely to be repeated in July 1984, in the hands of local groups. As part of the Aberystwyth summer festival in July 1983, Crosville's preserved Bristol SC4LK operated a town tour in Aberystwyth, incorporating amazingly tight streets in the old part of the town. There is speculation that the company's preserved Bristol L5G bus may be available to perform a similar tour by 1984. With or without its presence, mid Wales might be well worth a visit, and *Pass Cambria* and the Travel Planner available with it will certainly make for an even more productive and economical visit.

PASS CAMBRIA

# All Types a driving experience with FF 20536

Most schoolboys harbour early ambitions to drive a railway engine, pilot a plane, or captain a ship, whilst no doubt modern youth has more exotic thoughts associated with space travel. My own desires were considerably more modest, and as a life-long bus enthusiast my adolescent thoughts were naturally orientated towards eventually steering a live psv. Some very marginal success had been accomplished during one school holiday by gaining access to the cab of an ancient ex-Hebble Albion half-cab which had been put out to grass. Thus numerous cycle rides were made to the 'old lady' with considerable imaginary miles of guiding the veteran through the Suffolk lanes by wrestling with the wooden steering wheel and effecting an excessive number of gear-changing operations. Imagine the disappointment on one such expedition to this super full size 'toy' to find the site cleared. Enquiries via the owner's ever helpful fitter revealed that the old bus had gone forever. The pangs of remorse were akin to similar feelings that youngsters have when deprived of the company of a dog or pony.

A five year apprenticeship as a structural draughtsman with associated attendance at college seemed to be a move even further away from my transport interests. However this very employment was instrumental in attaining my goal. One afternoon while left in charge of the office – all the other members of the staff were out – the proprietor of a bus and coach company called with a view to negotiating a parking area on my employer's land. Seeing the type of work I was engaged upon he requested me to visit him to view a new town site he had bought for his expanding fleet some three miles from his then village base. This meeting resulted in the preparation of drawings for planning applications in exchange for a training exercise for a psv licence.

An appointment was fixed for 9am one Sunday for an initiation into the complexities of guiding a bus along the highway. Anxious to sample the delights of the experience I arrived precisely on time, but, lest I needed moral support I took my younger brother along for the ride and perhaps the laughs. Gentle knocking the door produced no response, so a lengthy press on the bell was tried. At this point an upstairs sash window slid down to reveal a pyjama-clad male figure holding his head. The expression was not the result of a hangover but indicated that he had overlooked our arranged timing. His rapid reappearance at the front door minutes later revealed that only shoes, trousers and jacket had been added to the apparel seen earlier at the window!

An ex-Suttons Leyland Tiger PS1/Duple coach duly came on to the forecourt of the site emerging from buildings, all of which had been recorded by myself on various documents. Thus the scene was set for my first half-cab mission. The Tiger gearbox whilst cold changed up through the range akin to a large heavy car, but alas, when requested to change down a few miles later the warm gearbox oil had thinned and the exercise was neither easy nor pleasant on the ears. A backward glance through to the passenger compartment revealed my two 'passengers' rocking with mirth; the type of reaction which did nothing for my rapidly sinking confidence!

Having been shown professionally how to effect upward and downward changes with minimum effort and without the attendant cacophony of grating, all apparently that was needed was in-tune practice. Therefore, every Sunday morning an uncomplaining brother gave concise yet blunt opinions of my limited progress. After many weeks with little or no improvement the proprietor decided to 'hot-up' the training. Our jolly jaunts through the Suffolk countryside in the coach ceased in favour of intensified tuition in the methods of accurate reversing, in an ex-Eastern Counties Leyland PD1/ECW with which I developed a love-hate relationship. Eventually I was considered to be a possibility for an MOT driving test, even after the unfortunate incident with the lorry.

I work on the assumption that if you have to have an accident, have it soon and get it over with quickly. While leaving the home base town through the narrow medieval streets of timber-structured houses with overhanging eaves, a large articulated lorry was observed coming towards us. The speed of both vehicles had dropped to a walking pace as we drew level in an attempt to slide past each other, which was partially achieved. Unfortunately a rope tie-off hook on the truck caught a lower deck window upright on the side of the bus which caused the window to break with an alarming bang. The only way to avoid further damage to the bus was to jack the lorry up to lift his line of hooks clear. This exercise blocked the main road into the town from the A12 for almost an hour. On my next appearance at the bus garage I was greeted with a grin from one of the fitters who enquired if I had called for a job as the window-cleaner!

The test itself is another traumatic affair as all novice car drivers will testify; similar antics with a lumbering great bus are even more nerve-wracking. The most horrific exercise was to be requested to change down through each gear ratio whilst descending a steep hill. The feet need to depress all three pedals to slow the vehicle down, disengage the clutch, and build up the revs to an alarming crescendo, and even with handbrake assistance the manoeuvre is ear and nerve shattering. Once completed, the examiner requested an immediate upward change; obviously he did not enjoy the screaming either! One unexpected happening during my ordeal occurred whilst driving up through *Coronation Street* style housing in the dockland area where a nappy-clad baby was sitting in the road. I slowed down, pulled into the side, stopped, applied the handbrake and was about to kill the engine, when a woman suddenly ran into the road, scooped up the child, raised her hand as a thankyou gesture and disappeared equally rapidly.

The promise of a plastic button hole badge via the GPO filled me with delight, whilst at the first set of traffic lights on my return to base, the kangaroo leaps of a learner car driver gave me the chance to assume a superior grin. This was dispelled on arrival back on the garage forecourt. The resident comedian/fitter noted my thumbs-up sign and retorted with a remark about the apparent reduction in the required standards. Now that I have notched up as many years psv driving as he had at the time, perhaps I can now begin to levy the same remarks at the new generation of trainees weaned on semi-automatic vehicles, known locally as 'Teflon' drivers (ie non-stick!)

As soon as the coveted red-edged badge arrived, I was allocated a private hire duty conveying an amateur Suffolk football team to an Essex village that ironically was later to be my home for seven years. The team lost their game, and I note in recent times they have now acquired their own coach. Hopefully it was not influenced by that journey made by any parent of the present team 18 years ago! My second private hire was more involved, working on hire to another Suffolk coach company to convey the then renowned HMS *Ganges* gymnastic display team to the Harlow New Town annual gala day. All went well on the outward trip via Key Glassworks, who provided an excellent lunch for both team and driver. At 11pm at the conclusion of all activities, my steed, a petrol Bedford SBG/Duple churned over well but despite

*Left:* **The 'battle of the box' began on one of these 1946 Leyland Tiger PS1 with Duple 33-seat bodywork, new to Suttons, of Clacton.**

*Above:* **The 'beast' in which the author passed his psv driving test, an ex-Eastern Counties Leyland Titan PD1A with ECW lowbridge body, seen in 1966 outside East Bergholt depot.**

*Above:* **The ill-fated 17 CPL, Bedford SBG/Duple Vega ex-Conway Hunt, Ottershaw, with a distinct list to port at Dedham in 1966. It was to survive for exactly four more years.**

*Left:* **The same coach after the 1970 burn up from Brantham to Bergholt.**

*Right:* **'Spare duty day' and Tillings 9417, a 1970 Bristol RELH6G/Duple Commander poses at Ridgewell, Essex on its return from Newmarket in June 1974. Its registration was really HVW 241H – speed had removed the 2 digit.**

occasional coughs and splutters failed to start. The lads pushed the old girl round and round the field in good naval style but all efforts to get the engine to run but a few seconds . . . failed.

Thus I had notched up my first knock and experienced my first breakdown very early in my psv driving activities, bearing out my 'get it over quickly' philosophy. Fortunately, although faults developed with other vehicles, I was to avoid complete failures for many years, averaging only one per three years. Ironically, my pioneer machine was set to fail at a much faster average rate. Two years later she was ditched at Dedham while on a school contract, in an attempt to avoid a recklessly driven cattle truck. A further two years passed before she went on a destruction derby drive. She was burnt out twixt Brantham and Bergholt whilst limping home from a works contract with a repeat of the fault which had caused my delay at Harlow, a ruptured diaphragm in the lift pump. At the cremation ceremony the engine backfired through the carburetter and set the lino and trim around the bonnet alight so quickly that within five minutes the empty coach was ablaze from end to end. One fact was certain, that vehicle never let me down again, so I viewed the burnt out framework without remorse. 17CPL RIP.

My next eventful trip began with the collection of a group of foreign students based at a large Suffolk farmhouse for a visit to Cambridge. All went well after the pick-up from the Arts Theatre until the first hill. The 7ft 6in wide petrol Bedford SBG showed distinct tiredness which increased as each slope was encountered until the last gradient into Haverhill when she began to boil merrily. Allowing the vehicle to take itself into the town (ie virtually no revs, just tick-over) we came to rest on Premier Travel's forecourt. After numerous phone calls to little avail, fortunately an AEC Reliance/Alexander arrived in off an express service. The friendly driver realised our plight and agreed to take my party back to the depot village. There I dug the sole remaining Bedford OB out, essential for the narrow roads back to the student's vacational farmhouse home. This was the last occasion that I used any petrol-engined vehicles on psv work.

Some full year after I had acquired my psv licence I was on one of my regular photo sorties to the largest local independent in my area, who by then I had known for over 15 years. On this occasion one of the sons of the proprietors expressed surprise at my continued interest in the fleet, yet I had not acquired a 'posy'. The term was a localism for a drivers badge which is perhaps obvious when worn in the lapel. The amazed look on his face when I told him I had an all-groups ticket spoke legions. From that day henceforth I was to be requested to do all types of work – stage, contracts, excursions and private hire. An equally diverse range of vehicles has led to a vast fund of travel experience.

An inter-school function took me to a school in the Clacton-on-Sea area with a well-laden Bedford YRT/Willowbrook bus, then so new it was still in dealer stock livery. On negotiating a large roundabout on the return journey an alarming metallic bang was heard amidships. The interior chatter ceased like magic, and in the moment of silence the master-in-charge enquired if the spare wheel had fallen off. The fact that it did not carry one plus the position of the temperature gauge needle suggested to me the fault lay elsewhere. From that moment onwards it was a case of Clacton Police Are Wonderful, for as my vehicle ground to a halt, the blue flashing light of a patrolman in a white noddy van was right up behind much to the delight of my youthful passengers. Radio link was made to police control who telephoned my operator's office; within half an hour my load had been transferred to a Ford R226/Duple returning empty from Clacton.

After a further half hour the patrolman suggested trying to drive the bus with considerably cooler power unit to a lay-by a few hundred yards away; this was principally to release the line of cones he had placed at the rear of the bus. I tried the starter, and she ran without any knocking. With a wave to my helpful lawman I set off and ran for five miles to the next village stopping at a telephone box to report my revised position. The guvnor suggested my taking it slowly into my home town and parking it up for collection by the breakdown crew. This was duly accomplished and I collected my long-suffering wife who had been waiting nearly two hours to go home for a rather belated tea.

Ironically, the next day I called at a Suffolk operator's premises with a destination blind to which I had added various additional stage

terminals. While I unloaded this item from my car boot I overheard one of their drivers telling the young guvnor how one of Osborne's part-timers had seized the water pump on a coach but had still driven the loaded vehicle all the way from Clacton back to the yard. I mused over the speed of the busman's canteen grapevine, coupled with the vastly inaccurate account of the facts. After the storytelling driver had gone beyond earshot I relayed the true account of the incident, which caused considerable mirth among the assembled management!

An unexpected phone call from an old school friend with an odd question was to change my driving lifestyle. His enquiry about the extent of my commitment to the independents made me curious about his reasons.

He explained that he was preparing a list of drivers suitable to help out in times of pressure. National Travel with part-timers? Unbelievable! I exploded. They preferred to call them Seasonal Drivers, a superior title for the same duty. I was invited to an initiation exercise, lengthy form-filling (totally alien to independents) and a test drive on two types of coach. A brand new Bedford YMT fresh in from Plaxtons was allocated for the stick box exercise, which being so new was extremely stiff to operate. A short ride in the lightweight met with approval, and a Bristol RE/Plaxton with semi-automatic gear selection was produced for evaluation. At that time my heavyweight coach driving activities had been limited to the AEC Reliance and the Leyland Leopard, so the opportunity to sample a rear-engined model was welcomed. The effortless cruising was sheer delight but my examiner insisted that a much faster average speed was required to maintain the express service timings.

I began to learn the ropes extremely quickly; while we were out on test the chartroom had rung in for a relief down from London. So without any more formality I was dispatched to Victoria with an RELH to work a duplicate down to Clacton-on-Sea. The regular service drivers were decent enough to give me a 'single drop' journey, ie loaded me up with Butlins Camp only, a familiar location which presented no routing difficulties. One early lesson I learned was to be cautious with the traffic office. They are ever anxious to get the work 'covered', and personal preferences are rapidly noted, eg I was foolish enough to say I liked working on the express service 084 Walton-on-Naze & Clacton-on-Sea to London (Victoria Coach Station) so I was allocated the same duty for five consecutive weeks.

Although this suited the clerical lads, the full-time drivers were anxious that no casual should

*Left:* **First trip out in 1976 for a National Bedford YMT/Willowbrook, seen at Mildenhall, Suffolk. Note the Willowbrook labels still in the destination box.**

*Above:* **At the Pollock Halls of Residence, Edinburgh University, one of three Youngs of Rampton coaches conveying mainly oriental students on a four-day Scottish visit in 1978. The coach is a Bedford YRT with Duple 53-seat Dominant Express body.**

latch on to anything too much of a doddle, so early or late duty was suggested. I elected to try the 6am sign-on, armed with correspondence to fight the eight hours of possible boredom in the driver's canteen. After the customary cuppa with the schedules man I consulted the output sheet, and dug out each required vehicle from the congested garage/yard prior to the allocated driver's arrival. This kept me amused for several hours, plus some additional shunting into the photographic corners of the yard for my own pleasures! It was during the first lull in activity when an anxious-faced senior member of the office staff approached me with a request to grab a fast spare motor and get to Chelmsford rapidly.

I selected an RELH, of course, with Duple Commander body – they had a depot reputation for being the flyers. I arrived at the bus station within 20 minutes to find two elderly ladies who had travelled by East Kent via the Dartford Tunnel, but had failed to make connection with a Norwich-bound coach. My task was to repair the faulty link with a rapid sprint to Bury St Edmunds, which involved passing through Braintree, Halstead and Sudbury on a busy Saturday. The uncomplaining passengers seemed to enjoy the speedy ride through the Essex/ Suffolk countryside, but imagine my dismay as I reached my destination to be greeted by a group of red buses with no white coach among them.

Phone calls from the duty inspector's office ensued. 'Take them to Thetford' was the first suggestion, promptly rejected by the Eastern Counties man as impractical. Then an alternative idea was offered after further consultation of the National Express' current volume – a quick dash down the A45 to Newmarket would give adequate time to connect with an alternative Norwich link. This was duly performed for the two long-suffering travellers who seemed to enjoy their bonus Anglian tour. I too found the entire journey exhilarating, particularly the return empty at a slightly more leisurely pace in what was a superb vehicle to handle. I had logged over 100 miles and accrued overtime by exceeding my 8hr duty. My enthusiasm to perform early spare driver again fell on deaf ears!

My four years on National were most enjoyable for the chance to sample different types of vehicles on an even greater variety of work. Tour feeders, partway express reliefs, weekends away on centred holidays, multi-vehicle private hires, around the capital on sightseeing tours with a London Transport guide – these were all types of work which had never previously been on offer. The stories are endless with lost luggage or just switched cases, rectified problems with embarrassing embraces are all part of the rich pageantry of a driver's life on the

Two DAF SB2300 with Berkhof bodywork at the Auchan Hypermarket in Boulogne, France in 1983.

nation's white coaches. I am convinced my career is all the richer for having had this major operator experience. One type of vehicle which I had no regrets about leaving behind was the Willowbrook Spacecar bodied coaches. Unpopular with the staff, even the general public were unimpressed for I well remember arriving at Dovercourt with a brand new example on a maiden trip to Windsor and public reaction was almost nil.

My full return to the private sector after the dissolution of National's South East coaching unit had the desired effect on the style of work and type of vehicle I was allocated. On the basis that I had driven all types, (which even included an AEC Regent V opentopper loaded with Round Table carol singers) on the full spectrum of work, apart from extended or continental tours and came through with an unscathed record. The news of any disciplinary action or accidental abrasion will circulate round driver's canteens and coach parks faster than any form of advertising or notice board can achieve! This is not usually generated in a malicious fashion, more of a jocular nature in sympathy with the luckless driver.

The vast majority of the psv/personnel that I have worked with have been a real friendly bunch, both in the National and independent sectors. There exists an unwritten fellowship symbolised by the friendly waves one receives from fellow psv drivers on the highway, and help is never far away. Assistance has no respect for distance either. When the National Travel (SE) closed, my contact took a similar post with a large coach operator in Cambridgeshire, some 50 miles away. I jokingly suggested he was completely out of range to help out now, but I had to eat my words! In less than a year I had worked on reliefs to Newcastle on hire to United, had a double-decker based in a sports complex near Ipswich and worked a four-day tour to Edinburgh. The Scottish job broke new ground for me, and added an unsavoury experience as my coach was broken into overnight, slightly soiling my opinion of an otherwise superb city.

The past 18 years of my life have been all the more colourful for having held a psv licence. Apart from the liveries of the vehicles driven, there has been the wealth of colours and creeds of the folks I have conveyed to an incredible variety of destinations. For those who are content to just watch or look on, but never touch, there is a world still unknown to them. The responsibility of a safe and enjoyable journey for a group of people is no burden to an enthusiast driver anxious to please. The gratitude of the departing passengers is always appreciated, giving one an exhilarating feeling as the vehicle is returned to base in the knowledge of another job well done. While my initial ambition has been fulfilled, there are still so many companies held in high regard, operating exotic vehicles to far away places that the opportunity to sample them is likely to remain but a dream, forever.

I pause, to answer the phone. A request to go as second driver on a day trip to Boulogne using a Berkhof-bodied DAF, the first in the country. Perhaps a Neoplan to the South of France is within reach in a few years, maybe?

# Cheltenham Departures

Photographs by T.W. MOORE

The mass departure of coaches from Cheltenham was a familiar part of the British coaching scene for nearly 50 years. Coaches converged from all parts of the country, passengers made their interchange, and the coaches set out again at 1430hrs (1500hrs in recent years). The growth of the motorway network and increase in coach speeds removed the need for the interchange, and the last mass departure took place in January 1984. These photographs were taken the previous August.

*Below:* Fond farewell before the lady boards a Lincolnshire Leyland Leopard PSU3E/3R with Plaxton 47-seat body, bound for Leicester.

*Above:* **Time for a chat as drivers wait for connecting services to arrive. The crews are Welsh, as is the National Welsh Leyland Tiger/Plaxton Paramount.**

*Left:* **One of the older coaches at Cheltenham, a much-travelled ex-Southdown Leyland Leopard/ Duple Commander working for Lincolnshire.**

*Right:* **Time to spare at Cheltenham between arriving and departing, and a chance to read the** *Daily Mail* **while waiting for the driver to load his luggage on a Welsh-bound journey.**

630 MILFORD HAVEN
BAY
7
353
NATIONAL EXPRESS
353
LEOPARD
KAD 353

*Left:* **Waiting by a Northern General Leyland Leopard with Willowbrook 003 dual-purpose body.**

*Below:* **Waiting for the driver. Having found their coach, would-be travellers wait for luggage to be loaded before boarding this Liverpool-bound National Travel West Leyland Leopard/Duple Dominant.**

*Left:* **A hired Clevedon Motorways Neoplan Cityliner noses out of Cheltenham Coach Station en route to Westward Ho!**

*Left:* **Two visitors from Scotland: a Western Scottish Seddon Pennine VII/Alexander T-type returning to Glasgow, and an Eastern Scottish Seddon/Plaxton Supreme continuing south to Truro.**

*Below:* **More continental variety at Cheltenham, a DAF with LAG Galaxy body from the Newbourne Transport fleet, working on hire on the 609 service to London.**

*Left:* **Waiting time for East Yorkshire driver Brian Andrew. Two more passengers are due to arrive on a connecting service from the south, before he can leave with his Leyland Tiger/ Plaxton Paramount.**

*Below:* **Loading up on the way to Paignton, a Yelloway Leyland Tiger with high-floor Plaxton Paramount 3500 bodywork.**

Right: On the 1500hrs departure to Wakefield and Leeds, a Wallace Arnold Volvo B58/Plaxton on hire to National Travel.

*Below:* **Inspector Len Williams sighs with relief as the last coaches file out of Cheltenham Coach Station on the 1500hrs departure on a busy holiday Saturday.**

# Taken Over: 3

*Above:* **Alexanders (Northern) bought Burnetts of Mintlaw in 1967. Included in the take-over was this AEC Reliance/Plaxton, new in 1958 to Shaw, Byers Green.**
*G.R. Mills*

*Below:* **When Western SMT took over the business of Paton of Renfew in 1979, ten Leyland Leopards passed into the Western fleet. Six had BET-style Willowbrook 53-seat bodies like KL5 seen here in Kilmarnock.**
*G. Coxon*

*Above:* **Although Scottish Omnibuses started to repaint the buses of Baxter, Airdrie in green following take-over in 1962, it recognised the local goodwill value and restored Baxter's blue. A Leyland PD2/10 with Massey body is seen in the short-lived light green livery.** *Gavin Booth*

*Below:* **Carmichael (Highland) of Glenboig passed to Alexanders (Midland) in 1966, and with it this Glasgow-style Leyland Titan PD3/2 with Alexander 72-seat bodywork, becoming the one normal-height double-decker in an otherwise lowheight fleet.** *G.R. Mills*

# Off the Rails

**STEWART J. BROWN in search of a train in Ecuador**

*'Hope springs eternal in the human breast'* – a train traveller in Ecuador.

This was originally conceived as a story for *Railway World Annual* but, as will become apparent as the tale unfolds, turned out to be a non-railway story – although trains do occasionally loom up in the background.

It starts in Quito. The story that is, most definitely not the train. A travel agent in Quito, the capital of Ecuador, offers a two-day trip by coach to Riobamba and from there by steam train to Guayaquil. Ideally the journey should be made in the reverse direction – which it can be – as Guayaquil is at sea level and Riobamba is 9,000ft up in the Andes. But for me logistics dictated a train trip down the Andes to Guayaquil as the first leg of a triangular tour embracing Quito, Guayaquil and Cuenca, the three biggest cities in Ecuador. That, at least, was the plan.

So, (as they say breathlessly on Radio 1 Newsbeat stories) I turned up at the tour departure point at 7.30am – an unearthly hour to be abroad when on holiday. Or to be on holiday when abroad. An assortment of fellow travellers were there too, as was the coach: an American Ford with 22-seat body built locally by Blue Bird Botar. My heart sank as I conjured up visions of a noisy trip in a small coach powered by a high-revving diesel engine. Had I brought my ear plugs? (Bought at Heathrow to isolate the noise of a plane-load of homegoing Latin Americans). But my visions were dispelled when the driver switched it on – 360cu in of V8 petrol power, as used in the biggest American Ford cars, whispered into life. A bit underpowered perhaps – the driver complained that it was lazy – but fairly quiet and with a delightful whine from first gear. All in all, a latter-day Bedford OB.

On route we stopped at Latacunga, a market town where buses outnumbered cars by about ten to one – there are a lot of buses in Ecuador. All those in Latacunga were based on bonneted American truck chassis and were petrol-engined. Bodywork was of local manufacture, often in cooperation with American builders of school buses like Blue Bird

*Left:* **A Toyota toils up the unmettaled main street of Chordeleg on the service from Gualaceo. The Andean backdrop is typical of the area.**
*All photos: Stewart J. Brown*

*Above:* **Narrow streets, steep hills and chronic traffic congestion characterise Quito. A Ford leads an International Harvester in an old part of the city.**

and Thomas. Liveries were colourful (a useful word to cover a multitude of indescribable colour combinations).

At Riobamba we stopped at the quaintly-named Hotel Galpon; a rough translation is 'badly constructed', although I've yet to have that verified by any of my English-Spanish dictionaries. If I had baulked at a 7.30 departure that morning you can imagine my horror when the guide announced a 4.30 call for the following morning – a little detail which the brochure had conveniently overlooked. We were assembled at 5.00, me and fellow travellers *sans bonhomie*, ready for the 150-mile trip to the coast behind a steam engine. At least the rain of the previous evening had stopped. My vocabulary of adjectives to describe increasingly heavy rain stops at torrential. The rain in Ecuador goes at least two stages beyond my vocabulary. Our guide had been making telephone calls and returned with an announcement: 'I have a bad new for you'. Well, at least it was only in the singular. (It's rather cruel of me to poke fun at her otherwise excellent English – you should hear my Spanish. But cruel I'm going to be). The 'bad new' was that the rain had caused a landslide. The 'good new' was that our first class carriage was in Riobamba station. The next bad news (plural after all) was that the locomotive wasn't. It was on the other side of the landslide, which it would probably take two days to clear. Could we get to Guayaquil by road? No. That was blocked too. What about the *autoferro*? (Railcar to you). No. It used the same track as the steam train – which I suppose should have been obvious. Could I get direct to Cuenca? No. Not from Riobamba. The group returned *en masse* to Quito on the little Ford coach without as much as the smell of a steam train.

At the travel agency's office in Quito I enquired about travelling direct to Cuenca; I wasn't too concerned about going to Guayaquil – it had just been a way-station on the train journey. There was one flight in the afternoon but Cuenca is surrounded by mountains and the airport is often closed when there is low cloud or heavy rain. There had been both that day. The only option was to remain in Quito or to fly to Guayaquil and catch a bus for a 150-mile trip to Cuenca. The plane to Guayaquil was a Caravelle. I remembered having read about the Caravelle when it was new and I was still at school – 25 years ago. Was I right to be surprised that any were still flying? Anyway it got me to Guayaquil, which is presumably fairly easy when you take off at 9,000ft and land at sea level and you

can do the aircraft equivalent of coasting downhill in neutral. And it cost only £9.20, the cheapest flight I've ever made. Guayaquil was hot (30 deg C) and sticky. A taxi took me to the terminal of one of the bus operators serving Cuenca.

The bus to Cuenca was fairly civilised, a 22-seat Mercedes diesel. The next departure was full. I was allocated a numbered seat on the following bus, an hour later. It was an express bus and the driver drove with verve. We stopped at three towns on the coastal plain and at each stop vendors of local delicacies (I use the term loosely) crowded round to offer their wares. Then we tackled the climb up the Andes. Following the rain, at various places land had been washed across the road without actually blocking it. At one spot half the road had disappeared further down the side of the mountain than I cared to look. But nothing deterred our demon driver. Mud on the road; low cloud; sheer drops down mountainsides – nothing slowed him down.

High in the mountains the driver's son collected money from some of the passengers. The bus stopped. All outside was damp and grey – more like the Scottish Highlands than the equatorial Andes. The boy leapt out and dropped the money in a box in front of a huge shrine by the roadside. Perhaps this explained the driver's supreme self-confidence on the dangerous Andean road . . .

By the time I reached Cuenca it was 7.30pm – 15 hours, one plane, one taxi and two buses since rising in Riobamba for a leisurely trip in a steam train. An impressive feature of the Guayaquil-Cuenca bus service was that each bus was washed before leaving Cuenca – not only impressive but also fairly necessary since dirt obscured most of the windows anyway.

Cuenca is Ecuador's third city and boasts a railway station. Having been thwarted in my first attempt to travel by train I went to the local tourist office and asked if it was possible to travel by train to Quito (some 280 miles distant). To say that the girls in the tourist office fell about laughing would be a gross exaggeration – but I got the message: it wasn't possible. The train from Cuenca was dependent on making a connection at Riobamba with the train from Guayaquil and if the train from Guayaquil failed to arrive there was no through journey to Quito . . . need I say more? How about a bus? A bus? *A bus*! Hysterics threatened. No. No bus. Only a choice of airlines – but the flight is dangerous. The runway is very short. There are mountains. The plane may not take off if it is raining. Three planes have crashed already this year . . . I wondered if my life insurance premiums were paid up to date.

In the style most people expect of eccentric foreigners I bought a ticket for the following afternoon's flight and then caught a bus to the railway station. The tourist office girl had told me which bus to catch and implied that it went near the

*Left:* **Latacunga has more buses than cars. At one of the many town centre loading points a collection of weary-looking buses is being prepared for departure.**

*Right:* **Sloping window pillars and whitewall tyres give this Ford a flashy appearance. The warning beacon on the roof must be the ultimate in one-upmanship. It is seen arriving in Latacunga from Umbato.**

station. Now, I know a little – possibly very little – about railways. I have seen small town railway stations in various countries and know not to expect grandiose buildings or great feats of engineering. Cuenca was a terminal and I anticipated finding a few sheds and at least a spare loco. I watched carefully as the bus neared the area where the tourist office girl had marked the station on the map. The bus – a bonneted Chevrolet, petrol-engined of course – abandoned tarred roads. Passengers abandoned the bus. Eventually it stopped in a sea of mud on the outskirts of the town. No sign of a station. I asked the driver in my halting Spanish 'Are we near the railway station?' 'Over there', he pointed. I looked. 'Over there?' I repeated stupidly. 'Yes, these little houses.' (A literal translation from the Spanish in which this quasi-conversation was conducted).

I picked my way carefully through the mud and yes – 'these little houses' were indeed the station. A few sheds? You've got to be joking. A spare loco? No chance. Only a derelict *autoferro*. I found a servant of the railway company. 'Sir!' I addressed him, 'at what hour does the train leave?' 'Six in the morning.' Further questioning elicited that it arrived at 7pm. I thanked him and was just leaving when he added: 'But it isn't running. Landslides have blocked the line. It'll be at least two days before it's clear.' Where had I heard that story before? And so back to central Cuenca and pictures of its rather ugly buses in its quaint and pretty cobbled streets.

From Cuenca I decided to visit Chordeleg, a mountain village which all tourists are urged to see for its crafts. This involved a hair-raising bus ride through narrow mountain passes, taking care to avoid boulders dislodged by the rain. At Gualaceo a change of buses from a 32-seat US Ford to a 22-seat US Ford which climbed a dubious unmade road to Chordeleg. The main street of Chordeleg looked like a nice spot for a bus picture. The driver assured me that there was a bus every ten minutes so I stood at the top of the street to wait for the next one. And waited . . . and waited . . . Ten minutes in Ecuador is half-an-hour anywhere else.

People carry interesting things on public transport in Ecuador. From Chordeleg a lady had a bucket full of hens' feet. On the plane from Cuenca to Quito a man had a live hen under his arm. Tables were loaded on roof racks (I'm back to the bus, not the plane). The flight back to Quito was uneventful despite the misgivings of the staff in the tourist office. To introduce a bit of culture to this tale, we even flew over Cotopaxi, one of the highest active volcanoes in the world, without it erupting.

In Quito I made one last desperate effort to see a train. It was now a matter of principle. The staff of tourist offices in Ecuador must by then have been wondering about the lunatic train traveller who never actually got on a train. I obtained directions to

*Left:* **Diesel-powered Mercedes run between Cuenca and Guayaquil. This is the Cuenca terminal of Super Semeria. Each bus is washed prior to its departure.**

*Left:* **Supetaxis provide the fastest intercity transport in Ecuador and are driven in a manner which suggests that speed is more important than safety. They have racy-looking bodies on light truck chassis – in this case a Ford. This is the village square, Chordeleg.**

*Below:* **Central Gualaceo, with the bus from Cuenca unloading. Note the well-loaded roof rack. Most of the route between the two towns is over unmade roads.**

*Right:* **The dead** *autoferro* **at Cuenca.**

the station and caught the inevitable petrol-engined bonneted bus. Quito is the hub, if such exists, of the Equatorian railway system and here at last was a station worthy of the name. Not exactly London Euston or Glasgow Central – not even Shepperton – but at least a station. But no trains. However all was not lost. The *autoferro* was due in at 6pm. That allowed time for a bus ride to the equator and then a crowded journey back to the station in the Quito peak on a 30-seat Chevrolet carrying over 60 people. Quito's main thoroughfare is crowded with buses throughout the day and at peak periods they form a continuous line moving at less than walking pace. Most are bonneted and most are petrol-engined – Chevrolet, Dodge, Ford, GMC and International Harvester. All are very cheap to buy and to run and are owned by cooperatives operating on different routes. A flat fare of 3p is charged. Body-swapping is commonplace with new chassis appearing under old bodies from earlier vehicles. Quito is served by as motley a collection of vehicles as I have seen, with none apparently bigger than 35 seats. European chassis are conspicuous by their absence and apart from the Mercedes midi-buses on the route from Guayaquil to Cuenca all I saw were a few bonneted Mercedes 911 in Quito and some Leyland Terriers in Guayaquil. Since my visit at the end of 1982 six Alexander-bodied Leyland Atlanteans have entered service on Quito's Avenida Amazonas, the Sauchiehall Street of Latin America.

I hadn't expected the *autoferro* to arrive at six and by the time my overloaded Chevrolet reached the station it was almost 6.30. I could hear the sound of a diesel engine as I entered the station. My heart beat faster. Success at last? No. Ecuador's railway system was able to snatch defeat from the jaws of victory. The *autoferro* was not expected before 8pm and my consolation prize was an uninteresting American diesel loco. By 8pm it would be dark. The next *autoferro* departure was at 6am the following day, when it would only just be light – so I wasn't getting up early for that. And so I left Ecuador . . . without seeing a steam train or an *autoferro*. Rightly or wrongly I still believe in their existence; I retain this irrational faith that trains do run in Ecuador even though I didn't actually see one.

My next plan? To visit Ecuador again, flying direct to Guayaquil, and to sit there in the station on a 24-hour vigil without sleeping until a steam train finally does arrive and to take the train to Riobamba and change there to the *autoferro* to Quito. In theory the trip should take two days (for under 300 miles!) Methinks I'd better allow two weeks.

# Omnibologitis

**'FFD' catches the bug**

Dear reader, I first became afflicted with 'Omnibologitis' at about the tender age of three (which was during the early war years) and the affliction has continued to this day. At that time I lived on a section of London Transport Country Bus route 301 which was also served by Eastern National.

One of my earliest recollections of buses was of an apparently driverless bus which conveyed me and my aunt home from Aylesbury. Later it was discovered that this was a London bus which had some of its windows boarded up following bomb damage, so it was not possible to see the driver from the rear of the lower deck. Another bus trip was to Stanmore (Middlesex) on an STL operating a Green Line route and I recall my father waving to stop the bus as it passed the house; the bus stopped just up the road and waited for us – in those days bus operators were still interested in carrying passengers. On this trip I was to see my first red LT buses (in quantity) working routes 142 and 158, and whilst waiting at Stanmore on the return journey an STD was seen coming down Stanmore Hill into the Broadway on route 142. I also recollect seeing trolleybuses entering Marsh Lane from London Road – was this a dispersal point to avoid having trolleybuses bombed in their depots?

'Omnibologitis' took a turn for the worse – in my parents' view at least – when I was given my first bus conductor's outfit on my fourth Christmas. It was not long after this that a change of schools became necessary (I had started school at the age of 3) as my school mistress had been called up for war service. She arrived at school in one of Eastern National's noisy Dennis single-deckers and informed us that the school was to close immediately; arrangements were then made for me to go to school at Tring. This meant travelling on London Transport ST-types on route 301 or Eastern National Bristol or Leyland vehicles on their Luton – Dunstable – Eaton Bray – Edlesborough – Ivinghoe – Tring – Aylesbury service. This helped me collect tickets for use with the bus conductor's set.

The Eastern National buses on the Luton – Aylesbury service were mainly Bristol K-type double-deckers with ECW lowbridge bodies of 1938-40 vintage, and older Leyland vehicles with (I think) Brush lowbridge bodies – some of which had roof route number boxes – supported by Dennis rear-

*Above:* **Waiting in Kingsbury Square, Aylesbury, a United Counties Dennis Lancet II with Willowbrook body.** *FFD*

entrance single-deckers with perimeter seating. Some of the Leylands received grey wartime livery. All these vehicles were driven at lively speeds compared with the sedate LT vehicles. The tickets issued were insert Setright printed on green card with the low values pre-printed eg 1d, 1½d, 2d and other values printed by the machine. However, my favourites were the bell punch tickets issued on some vehicles. I have reason to believe that staff operating from Aylesbury garage used Setright machines, and those operating from Luton used Williamson bell punches in conjunction with two or three long ticket racks. Some of these tickets are still in my collection bearing such messages as: 'THE ENEMY HAS LONG EARS Guard your conversation'; 'NEVER DISCUSS MOVEMENTS OF TROOPS OR SHIPS Dangerous Talk Costs Lives!'; 'After dark remember YOU CAN SEE A CAR WHEN THE DRIVER CAN'T SEE YOU'.

The ST-types operated on 301 were mainly of the LGOC type, but from time to time a Bluebird style ST would appear. On trips to relatives at Chesham, C-type Leyland Cubs worked 'over the hill' on route 397, or if one travelled via Berkhamsted one could travel from Berkhamsted to Chesham on the 353 on a forward entrance STL. Whilst waiting for connections at Berkhamsted it was possible to see a grey and red single-decker of the B&B company being driven by a woman driver. The vehicle concerned was forward-control layout and was operated on B&B's Potten End service.

A bus journey to my grandmother's at Wendover nearly always entailed a journey via Aylesbury where it was possible to travel by Eastern National (usually double-deckers), London Transport route 359 operated by 10T10 types with perimeter seating, or on a Bedford owned by Red Rose of the RR Garage, Wendover. Travel by Red Rose could be quite interesting, as it competed with Eastern National between Aylesbury and Halton Camp via Wendover; the driver would emerge from the Victoria Working Men's Club in Kingsbury Square, then the main bus terminal in Aylesbury, the fares would be collected and the money lobbed into a cash bag hanging from the windscreen opening arm (tickets were only issued for return fares) and a well loaded, perhaps overloaded bus would convey one swiftly to Wendover.

*Above:* **Green Line T624, a 1938 AEC Regal 10T10 type, waits at Eccleston Bridge, London, before departing for Aylesbury in January 1952. Within three months the Green Line RF types had arrived, and replacement of the T types commenced.** *Alan B. Cross*

It was at the time I was travelling to school at Tring that LT in its wisdom decided that the 301 should be operated by producer gas ST-types. The first journey ever made on one of these was one hot summer afternoon from Tring to Berkhamsted. Outside Tring garage, my mother and I boarded a red ST, which already had its two-wheeled gas trailer attached. We moved off sluggishly to the accompaniment of much back-firing until we reached the point in London Road where the 397 (now 394) route left the main road to go to Wigginton (and on to Chesham). By this time our driver had had enough, left his cab and poked the fire, resulting in some back-firing but an improvement in speed, so much so that we overtook a Bluebird ST going down Pendley Beeches (downhill needless to say) and by the time we had reached Berkhamsted the journey had become much quieter. A feature of travelling on these buses was the smell of coke/gas fumes and a sort of heat haze over the trailer. The change-over of trailers at Tring garage rarely seemed to go smoothly as it took much effort to coax the bus into life again.

About this time I think it was the Green Line withdrawal notices (printed in black on white paper) appeared on bus stops.

Tring garage always interested me as its Frank Pick style of design was very modern. During the war there was a large static water tank on the sloping forecourt on the same side as the office block, a brick-built shed being built in the garage yard to the left of the slope – I believe to hold the fuel for the producer-gas buses. Shortly before I left the school at Tring I saw Green Line 10T10 coaches which were still in khaki livery with a white star on their rear emergency doors; no doubt they were awaiting Chiswick overhaul. Other LT garages of modern design in the area included Two Waters (HH), Amersham (MA) and High Wycombe (HE).

However, to return to the war years, outings other than journeys to school or to visit relatives were few and far between. One outing that fascinated me was to Oxford on City of Oxford route 82, the fascinating piece being the run from the main road into Haddenham and back, a feature which I had not come across before. The tickets issued were printed by Williamson and were of the bell punch variety measuring just over four inches, with a tear-off return section. At this time Oxford also used Bellgraphic ticket issuing machines. Another outing was by Icknield Coaches of Tring, whose garage was situated at the junction of Miswell Lane and Upper Icknield Way in some corrugated iron sheds. I was with my local Cub pack to visit Scout headquarters in London. Apart from seeing various LT buses and trolleybuses, a feature of this visit was the discovery that boy scouts had helped man the trams in Birmingham during the 1926 General Strike and some of the badges etc were on display. Another discovery was the Q type vehicles operating LT route 387 from Tring to Tring Station; these buses seemed to me to have a sort of waddling motion and the strap-hangers (which I had not seen before) swayed with the motion of the bus. I was recently reminded of this feature when travelling on a Leyland National which had straps of very similar design. On the odd trip into London, Green Line TF type vehicles were to be seen on duty as ambulances, I also remember seeing the RT buses on a visit to London Zoo and for some odd reason I was able to recognise these buses by the ventilation louvres beneath the driver's cab window.

In 1945 I started going to school in Aylesbury, where were to be seen the buses of London Transport on routes 301 (Aylesbury – Watford) and 359 (Aylesbury – Great Missenden – Amersham); Eastern National with services to Amersham (route 359 joint with LT), Bedford, Halton Camp (via Wendover), Luton, Leighton Buzzard and various places to the east of Aylesbury; City of Oxford which ran to Oxford, Thame, Bicester and points north and west of Aylesbury; United Counties route 46 to Northampton (via Buckingham); Thames Valley to High Wycombe; Red Rover to Buckingham, Waddesdon and Weedon; Queens Park Coaches to Halton Camp (via Weston Turville); and Red Rose to Halton Camp (via Wendover).

Two other operators not yet mentioned were Rover Bus and Lee & District which operated routes from Chesham, although it must be said that my clearest memories of these operators date from shortly after the war. The Rover fleet consisted mainly of Dennis and Bedford vehicles, and the Lee & District service always seemed to be operated by a Bedford with Mulliner body.

The LT and Eastern National vehicles have already been described. Thames

*Right:* **London Transport Country Area STL2666 on route 362 at Chesham Broadway in October 1949. This was an 'unfrozen' vehicle, completed during wartime.** *Alan B. Cross*

*Right:* **Early in 1953 green London Transport RLH48 waits at Berkhamsted Station before returning to Windsor on non-RLH route 353. RLH48, new in 1952, had a Weymann 53-seat body on AEC Regent III chassis.** *FFD*

ASTORIA
schweppervescence
lasts the whole drink through
WISK
362A HOLMER GRN AMERSHAM CHESHAM
HIGH WYCOMBE
GOODWINS BAR
CHEMIST
LONDON TRANSPORT
FXT 389

WINDSOR BUS STN
353 CHESHAM AMERSHAM
RUSSELL THOMAS
7 13 19 MARKET STREET WATFORD
Specialists in
GOOD FURNITURE
BEDDING CARPETS
RLH 48
LONDON TRANSPORT
MXX 248

*Above:* **An ex-Eastern National Bristol K5G of 1940 vintage, with ECW 48-seat lowbridge body, seen after transfer to United Counties, who acquired the Eastern National midland area services and fleet on 1 May 1952. It waits on the forecourt of the Cosy Corner Cafe, Aston Clinton, whilst the driving trainees and instructor enjoy a quick cuppa.** *FFD*

Valley also employed Bristol double-deckers and on odd occasions, Leyland double-deckers were to be seen – in some cases with open stairs. Later I discovered Leyland single-deckers were used on route 80 (Aylesbury – High Wycombe via Longwick, Lacey Green). United Counties also ran Bristols (this company used the Willebrew ticket system). Red Rover operated utility Daimler double-deckers and Dennis saloons in its famous biscuit and dark carnation red livery. Red Rose operated normal control Bedfords, and Queens Park Coaches operated Leyland and Dennis single-deckers based at a garage in Walton Road, Aylesbury, which was also used as City of Oxford's outstation.

The summer of 1946 was certainly the 'Year of the Bus' for me. On an outing to Amesham I noticed some 10T10 coaches on Amersham garage forecourt in shiny new Green Line livery. The Green Lines were back! My own local routes, 706 (Aylesbury – London – Westerham) and 707 (Aylesbury – London – Oxted) were among the last to be introduced. Later two more routes were noted, 724 (High Wycombe – London) and 725 (Chesham – London), both operated by 6Q6 type vehicles; these routes were later to form the northern sections of 709/710 and 711 respectively. Later in 1946 I was to go on holiday to Bournemouth and trolleybuses galore! Hants & Dorset buses were seen at various points from Winchester onwards on the journey south, and my first ride on a bus in Bournemouth was by Hants & Dorset. However, after pestering my parents they eventually agreed to return to our hotel at Westbourne by Corporation trolleybus. We boarded one of the famous Sunbeam MS2 trolleybuses at the Square for my first trolleybus ride and it was on this journey that the once familiar rear entrance/front exit arrangement was experienced – the front exit being opened by a 'grab and pull' mechanism operated by the driver. Other services passing the hotel were BCT routes 6 and 17 operated by prewar Bedfords with Burlingham bodies, having both driver and conductor. A visit was made to Christchurch and the famous trolleybus turntable was seen for the first time. I recall the fare was 6d (2½p) adult from the Square to Christchurch. On a number of occasions journeys were made on the petrol-engined Leyland TD5 vehicles, with their upper deck sunshine roofs open. It was sometime before I realised that the quiet ride was due to the petrol engine, unlike the harsher Leyland diesel of the local Eastern National buses. Another local feature that interested me was seeing Royal Blue vehicles leaving the basement of the bus station for distant places in the evening, and wondering how long their journeys would take.

The high spot of this particular summer was a visit to my cousin in London, who was a trolley-bus driver with LT at Stamford Hill. We travelled to Watford on the 301, then 306 from Watford Junction to Barnet and thence by trolleybus to Amhurst Park via Finchley and Wood Green. On the first evening we went to see Tower Bridge being raised, and prior to the return journey the driver of the vehicle we had boarded showed me what he had to do to change over from overhead power collection to battery operation. During this time I saw a fair amount of London, my first tram ride was made from Blackfriars Bridge to Westminster Bridge, and later excursions involved travelling on the Subway routes. What

an experience rushing down into the tunnel from the Bloomsbury end; I found the noise and bucking and swaying of the tram over what appeared uneven track – quite frightening. The conductor, who signalled the driver to stop and start by blowing a whistle – at all stops, opened the door at the top of the front stairs to allow passengers to alight via the driver's platform at the stations in the Subway which had island platforms only between the two tracks. One feature I remember well was sitting on the curved seat at the rear of the tram and watching the trolley rope swinging with the movement of the tram. A visit was made to Stamford Hill depot to obtain yet more tickets for a later edition of the bus conductor's outfit which now included a proper ticket rack. A large paper sack was used to accept the contents of the used ticket boxes of the trolleybuses as they ran in. A piece of equipment called a traverser was seen, a platform which was mounted in a pit running the length of the depot. The traverser was controlled by means of a tramcar-style controller and incoming trolleybuses were driven on to the platform which took the vehicle bodily sideways to the point where it was to be washed and then driven to the other end of the depot where it was either parked or taken to its parking place on the traverser. Mother was not pleased with the vast increase in ticket stocks and shortly after most of them mysteriously disappeared!

An operator not yet mentioned was Keith Coaches which ran a fleet mainly consisting of AEC vehicles. My first outing with this firm was to Wickstead Park, Kettering in a normal control Morris-Commercial with opening sunshine roof. Other outings were made regularly to the pantomime at the New Royal Theatre, Oxford and I recall that usually AEC Regal III were used, these having either Duple or Plaxton bodies. Later still, outings were made to Bournemouth, when not only the Regal IIIs were used but older vehicles also operated on these outings including on one occasion an aged petrol-engined Regal with characteristic hissing engine.

In the early postwar years the Icknield fleet consisted of recent

*Above:* **The author's favourite Eastern National type, a Leyland Titan PD1 with ECW 53-seat lowbridge body. It is seen on service 7D (Bedford-Stony Stratford-Buckingham-Finmere-Bicester-Oxford), operated jointly with City of Oxford.** *R.H.G. Simpson*

Bedford OB/Duple 29-seaters, an aged AEC Reliance, and two Guy coaches, one of which I think had a Meadows engine. In addition there was a Bedford WLB.

It was during this time that the Tilling companies (including Eastern National) were receiving their first postwar vehicle deliveries. In fact the Eastern National Midland Area timetable was interspersed with small adverts apologising for the use of old vehicles and saying that new ones were being introduced. The vehicles being delivered were the increasingly familiar Bristol K and L types with ECW bodies, but one batch which became my favourites were the Leyland PDI buses with ECW bodies. At this time the old prewar Leylands received new ECW bodies, a fate to which the older Bristol double-deckers were also subjected. Eastern National took over Red Rose, and also Queens Park Coaches (the latter in 1952), but the big event so far as Eastern National was concerned was when United Counties took over its Midland area on 1 May 1952.

Eastern National experimented with the now familiar Setright Speed ticket issuing machine circa 1947/48, and this machine differed slightly from production models in that it seemed that there were fewer dials and a noticeable feature was that the ticket roll was not fully enclosed.

One of my aunts went to live in Brighton just after the war, and on a number of occasions I went there to stay. My first visit was in 1947 (maybe earlier) when the Brighton, Hove & District company could still field large numbers of Tilling ST type vehicles with open stairs. Then there were the four-wheel trolleybuses of Brighton Corporation which took me to my aunt's. In those days Brighton buses were painted red and cream, and looked very smart. In later years the BH&D ST vehicles were to be seen rebodied with ECW or Beadle bodies, but with TT Co Ltd on their radiators; my cousin and I christened these buses 'Thomas Tilling crates' which I think summed them up. On these buses the bell code was posted in the cab, and therefore the driver was in no doubt as to what the conductor was signalling. There was also the interesting Southdown fleet with single-deckers having the unusual feature of destination displays in the side cant panels and in the lower rear panels. Later BH&D was to take delivery in large numbers of standard Bristol K-type with ECW highbridge bodies; Southdown postwar deliveries included Leyland PD Titan, PS Tigers and the rare Leyland Royal Tigers with East Lancs rear entrance bodies. Among my favourites on the Brighton scene were the Corporation AEC buses – both prewar and postwar.

On July 21 1948 I took my first ride on a postwar RT (RT 600) which had been delivered to Tring the previous evening along with RT 597, 598 and 599, all of which had roof route number boxes. Prior to the RTs being delivered some Tilling STL buses were operated on 301 initially in red livery, later being repainted green. Another type to appear at Tring was the CR which replaced the Q types on route 387. On outings to London and other places in LT territory it was clear that the RT family was appearing in large numbers. Other later changes in the LT scenery were the delivery of lowbridge RLH buses to Amersham for the 336 in place of the familiar lowbridge STs. Outings with bus spotter friends took me to Watford where RTWs were at work on 142 and 158; into London where there were still LT, ST, STL, D, B, G, T, TF, C, TD and STD buses as well as trolleybuses and trams to be seen: and I recall a trip to Kingston where 'Diddler' trolleybuses were still operating. Festival of Britain year, 1951, saw the arrival of the RFW and private hire RF vehicles, and at Easter 1952 on a homeward journey from a holiday at Brighton, I travelled on a newly-delivered Green Line RF and was impressed with the smooth ride.

Shortly before leaving school I had the privilege of gaining entry to Tring garage, when a school friend of mine (whose father was the garage inspector) arranged for us both to see 'Ole Bill' (B43) when it visited the garage. The old bus was to be used at the funeral of one of the drivers who had died. Shortly after seeing the bus in the garage I saw it proceed to Aylesbury (at a sedate speed) for the funeral, and was impressed as to how quiet the vehicle was.

The family took regular holidays at Bournemouth in the years between 1946 and 1952, and during the course of these holidays we travelled on half-day tours operated by Charlie's Cars, whose fleet was mainly Albion but included some Bedford vehicles. Charlie's Cars depot, a scene of much shunting of vehicles at certain times of the day, was right opposite the hotel. In

fact the hotel has since been demolished to make way for a new road, and the garage is now a tyre depot. We made tours into the New Forest and to Southampton in the immaculate maroon and cream coaches – usually Albions. On a couple of occasions Southampton trams were to be seen, the majority having the domed Bargate type roofs, and most of these vehicles were seen near the Royal Pier where the coach picked up and set down. On one trip I recall being held up by traffic and seeing an open-fronted tram pass in the opposite direction. Other Bournemouth coach operators at this time were Excelsior European Motorways and Shamrock and Rambler (orange and cream livery), the latter firm operating Bedford OB vehicles with Duple bodies and later progressed to Bedford SB coaches with Gurney Nutting bodies.

Some journeys were made into the Purbecks (usually by car) and to Swanage via Hants and Dorset service 7 and the Sandbanks Ferry. These excursions resulted in the discovery of Southern National which operated double-deck buses (well loaded) in the Wareham, Swanage, Corfe Castle and Lulworth areas.

On some occasions holidays of days out were the norm. One memorable outing in the summer of 1949 was to Banbury, Stratford-upon-Avon and Evesham returning via Oxford. I was already familiar with Midland Red coaches which operated through the village on service J (Birmingham-Banbury-Aylesbury-London), but I was to see large numbers of the buses built by this famous company, like SOS, FEDD, ON types as well as some more modern examples. Also at this time Stratford-upon-Avon Blue Motors was still operating Tilling-Stevens Express saloons. A souvenir of this outing which I retained for some years was the Midland Red Worcester Area timetable obtained from the company's Evesham office for the immense sum of 4d (roughly 1½p) which I considered excellent value for a book which was about an inch thick. One lasting memory of Evesham was seeing a large number of early BMMO single-deckers waiting under the trees (on the same side of the road where the buses still park).

Variety was produced in the summer months on the J service when not only were Midland Red C and ONC type coaches were to be seen, but they were joined by BMMO underfloor-engined buses and East Kent, Southdown and Maidstone & District half-cab vehicles working through to Birmingham from the South Coast resorts.

Early in 1953 the family left Buckinghamshire to take up residence in Bournemouth, and your author was to make his entry into the bus industry shortly after. That, however, is part of another story.

*Above:* **A Leyland Tiger PS1 with Park Royal 32-seat rear entrance body, typical of the East Kent express fleet in the early postwar years. It is working its way to Birmingham on a through service from the south-east in June 1952.**
*Alan B. Cross*

# Taken Over: 4

*Above:* **In 1973 Hants & Dorset bought the business of R. Chisnell (King Alfred) of Winchester, along with several buses including this Plaxton-bodied Leyland Panther PSUR1A/1R.** *G.R. Mills*

*Below:* **This Guy Arab IV with Massey bodywork was the last new bus delivered to and operated by Moore Bros. of Kelvedon before the company was acquired by Eastern National in 1963. At Chelmsford railway station in 1973, it has the Johannesburg-style front.** *G.R. Mills*

*Right:* **Tillingbourne (Metropolitan) AEC Reliance/Duple Dominant JTM 109V with a good load at Addington on the Forestdale service.** *All photos: Michael Dryhurst*

# Independence from the Monopoly

**MICHAEL DRYHURST on new faces in London**

Despite the fact that the London Passenger Transport Act of 1933 created a monopoly area for the then newly-created London Passenger Transport Board, an anomalous situation immediately existed whereby certain operators still retained pick-up rights within the so-called 'monopoly area'. Companies such as Birch Bros and Thames Valley spring to mind, as does the 251 service of the City Coach Co from Wood Green to Southend, which later passed to Eastern National, this last-named operator also working a stage service from Bow, Tomlins Grove, to Chelmsford, which in later days was serviced by double-deckers. Down in the south-western corner of LT's Central Area, Walton-on-Thames Motor Services provided a stage service from their garage in Bridge Street (now the local Volkswagen dealership) to Walton Station which ran right within LT territory but survived the 1933 Act, until 1970. Since the mid-1950s a number of stage operators has taken to the roads of the LT area, and this is a brief summary of some of those operations.

Working clockwise from the Thames Estuary, the first operator that we encounter is **Thames Weald Ltd**, of West Kingsdown, Kent. Although the major portion of its operations is within the area served by London Country Bus Services, Thames Weald has a trunk route right into LT land. The company started in 1962 and developed a network of routes centred on West Kingsdown to the main shopping centres of the area, such as Dartford, Gravesend and Sevenoaks, plus a cross-Thames service via the Dartford-Purfleet tunnel, having for many years now provided the only such service since the withdrawal of LT 300 and 722, although Eastern National 402 has six daily journeys via the tunnel. The Thames tunnel service is the main Thames Weald route from West Kingsdown to Romford, and at one time this had a two-hourly headway with certain journeys extended southward to Crawley via Edenbridge and Gatwick, whereas operation is now confined to Wednesdays, Fridays and Saturdays, the Crawley licence having been surrendered early in 1978. In October 1978 there was a traffic court hearing to decide the future of Thames Weald operations; had the Commissioners decided against the licences being renewed, London Country was going to step in with Dartford-Romford route 482, but in the event, Thames Weald was successful.

The company has used always small vehicles with a limited seating capacity, there having been nothing bigger than 29-seaters. All buses carry considerable anti-smoking propaganda, and they usually have hand-painted route details above the windows. In December 1980 the company put into service a Dodge 23-seater wherein was inscribed this notice to customers – 'This is *your* bus. Look after it, as you won't get another new one for years!'

Still in Kent, **Thamesmead Motor Services Ltd**, which has been associated with a number of stage services in south east London, took over operation in July 1975 of a service previously run by Belvedere Coaches in the Crabtree Manor Way Industrial Estate. The Thamesmead service ran between Belvedere Station and the Estate, half-hourly, Mondays-Fridays peak hours.

Another Kent operator to emerge in the 1960s was **North Downs Transport**, which started some services in the Orpington area after LT route reductions, as did **Orpington Rural District Transport Association**. A further operator on the Kent scene was **Orpington & District Omnibuses**, which operated a route from the Forestdale Estate to Croydon that it had inherited from the building firm of Wates, who had worked a minibus service over the route during the time that the estate was being developed. Orpington & District gradually absorbed routes from the other operators until it had seven in operation, with numbers between 853 and 861. However, none of these services received any sort of subsidy and financial losses coupled with a severe shortage of crews led to the withdrawal of two routes in the summer of 1977, and all operations on a Saturday came to an end in July 1980. The proprietor, Miss Normington, suffered a prolonged illness during the latter part of 1980 and in July 1980 service reductions were said to have been instituted because of falling traffic due to the high levels of fares imposed by LT, higher than Orpington wished to charge and higher than their passengers wished to pay. All of these events had a profound effect on the business, with the Biggin Hill 858 being withdrawn in December 1980 because the two Ford A0609 minibuses used on the route were unserviceable. The 'prime' 853/855/857 routes to East Croydon station were reduced to operation in peak hours only as from February 16, 1981 and a week later were cut even more drastically to just operation of the 855 (Croydon-Forestdale), again only in peak hours. Unfortunately, the last serviceable bus failed after morning duty on February 27, and to all intents and purposes the company no longer operated. The evening peak service was taken over by the well-known Surrey independent **Tillingbourne Bus Company** of Gomshall, and on March 2 this company resumed a full peak hours service, reconstituting operations with a subsidiary company known as **Tillingbourne (Metropolitan) Ltd**. The basic route structure was retained, with

*Left:* **The Thames Weald Dodge midibus lays over at Romford after working the 'Tunnel Express' from Sevenoaks. Fairly luxurious seating for 23 people is provided in what the proprietor describes as "your last new bus for years".**

*Right:* **A Weymann-bodied Leyland Atlantean of Orpington & District arrives at the East Croydon terminus of route 851. This particular bus was ex-Ribble, similar examples in the O&D fleet coming from Maidstone & District.**

the Orpington & District route numbering having the '8' prefix replaced by a '3'. In June 1981 the pick-up/set down restriction between Keston Mark and Orpington was lifted by LT, allowing competition with that operator's route 61, whilst in November of that year the Croydon services were extended to Fairfield Halls, giving better facilities for shoppers. June 1982 saw the introduction of a service from Orpington to Brighton marketed as Coastlink, whilst the Sanderstead-Addington-Bromley 354 came into being during the same month.

Vehicle policy in Orpington & District days had been to use maximum capacity saloons, but some ex-Maidstone & District Leyland Atlanteans with lowheight Weymann bodies were acquired and used extensively on the Croydon routes. Tillingbourne employed single-deckers initially, mainly using AEC Reliances but in the spring of 1982 an ex-West Yorkshire Road Car Co. Bristol VRT double-decker, painted as an all-over advertisement for a supermarket chain, came into the fleet.

Orpington 858 was taken over by **Crystal Coaches**, operating Orpington-Downe-Biggin Hill with Ford A0609 PPP 145R, with the route number painted on to the front and rear roof panels.

**Banstead Coaches Ltd**, from the Surrey town of that name, operated at one time two stage services in that area, albeit unconnected. The Chipstead Valley to Banstead service started in 1959 whilst in 1964 the company provided a replacement for the short-lived LT 263 with a service from Coulsdon North to The Mount, operating it until March 31, 1980. In July of that year it was taken over by **Tandridge Taxis** and numbered 26B, which happened to be the number of the company's office. However, Tandridge ceased operation on the Coulsdon Woods – The Mount route on March 27, 1982 and although residents of the area hired a bus on the two following days, the area remained bus-less thereafter. The Chipstead Valley service of Banstead Coaches continues, usually operated by a Willowbrook-bodied Bedford YRQ.

In the London Borough of Richmond **Continental Pioneer Coaches** provided a service from Richmond Station to Richmond Hill, which at one time was LT route 235 and never reinstated after an overtime ban that necessitated service cuts. Retaining the same route number, **Isleworth Coaches** provided a replacement service using an ex-LT RTL, operation passing to Pioneer in May 1968. The Hill terminus was at Cardigan Road which meant that buses had to undertake a very awkward three-point reverse turn, an operation that was eased when the route was extended in 1976 in a loop over the Hill, via the Star and Garter home and Marchmont Road. With virtually no warning the company ceased to operate on the route from September 27, 1980 and the 235 was replaced by diverting LT 71 over the Hill. Pioneer had used a

*Right:* **The first bus bought by Ben Stanley Ltd on the occasion of the company's return to stage operation was this Bedford VAS1 with 29-seat Marshall body, seen at Walton Centre when new.**

*Below:* **Walton-on-Thames Motor Co. Bedford OB lays over at Walton Station on the service thence to Walton Bridge, which survived the 1933 London Passenger Transport Act.**

*Facing page:* **In 1969 Golden Miller of Feltham bought a new bus, this Bristol LH6L with Plaxton body, seen at Shepperton passing the Ian Allan office, Terminal House.**

vast assortment of buses on the route, including RF, RT and RTL, an ex-Thames Valley Bristol LL6B and various coaches, although the stalwart in latter years was a Ford R192/Willowbrook bus, appropriately numbered PGX 235L.

LT service cuts formed the basis of **Mole Valley Transport Services** network. A Cobham to Downside route was opened in the autumn of 1968 at a time when LT still reached the former point with the 215, and in 1971 the company took its present title. A number of routes was inaugurated but the anticipated traffic failed to materialise resulting in many route withdrawals, such as Cobham to Walton-on-Thames and Cobham to Epsom. Withdrawal of London Country route 416 between Leatherhead and Esher led to Mole Valley route 1, whilst route 2 is Oxshott-Cobham-Downside. In 1979 market day services to Guildford and Kingston respectively were applied for, these commencing operation early in 1980, and also in that year the familiar withdrawal of Saturday services occurred, in March. In September 1980 LT withdrew its 201 Kingston-Surbiton-Hampton Court service and that section of the 215 between Lower Green and Hampton Court; Mole Valley replaced these with its Esher-Hampton Court-The Dittons-Surbiton route 7 on September 29. The Guildford route was axed in 1981 and in July of that year a reshuffle of routes took place, including the extension of 7 to Kingston. The company has always used minibuses, although a Rootes-bodies Dodge midibus was owned in the late 1970s.

**Ben Stanley Ltd** of Hersham started business during the 1920s, and amongst other activities operated a bus service between Hersham and Weybridge, but this was lost to London Transport under the 1933 Act, and so the company must have felt more than a sense of poetic justice when it took over operation of the southern end of LT 264 in January 1978. Numbered route 1, it works from

Walton Centre to Hersham, but proceeds beyond the former LT terminus at The Green to the company's garage in Burwood Road. At the beginning of the winter school term in September 1980 the company introduced a schooldays service between West Molesey and Esher via East Molesey and Lower Green, and when in November 1981 Surrey County Council withdrew support for LT 152A, which was basically a schools service, Ben Stanley filled part of the void with its route 2, a schoolsday service from Hook to Hampton Schools via Kingston by-pass and Hampton Court. Initially the company used a coach on the Walton service, but in June 1978 a Bedford VAS1 with Marshall B29F body was purchased, joined by a Bedford YMT with Duple B55F body in early 1980.

One of the best-known of the stage operators in the LT area must be **Golden Miller Services** of Feltham, by virtue of the fact that one of its routes passes the Ian Allan headquarters at Shepperton. The present company has existed since 1967, having inherited a stage service between Feltham Station and Bedfont that was started in 1955 by West London Coachways using a Bedford OB with Duple B29F bodywork, the first such route to be started within the LT Central Area since 1933. In February 1968 two new routes over previously unserved areas were introduced, one to Shepperton Station via Ashford Common and the film studios, the other being a Hanworth circular, both routes starting from Feltham Station being numbered respectively 602, 603, the Bedfont route becoming 601. With the cessation of the previously-mentioned service to Walton Station, Golden Miller took over the route in January 1970, numbering it 604; it was later extended to Oatlands Village but lack of patronage led to its withdrawal in 1974. Mole Valley provided a partial replacement, but only until November 1975. Walton Station has been served for a number of years now by LT 218 diverting off the main route at Halfway and doing a double run to and from the station. The Staines to Stanwell service, divorced from the rest of the GM routes based on Feltham, was introduced in November 1971 eventuallly becoming 606, but this route has encountered some considerable competition of late, from LCBS 436, and to a lesser extent 455, 456.

A mixed fleet of buses is operated. At the time of writing this includes 3 Bedford YRQ and a Bristol LH6L, all carrying Plaxton bus bodies and purchased new; a B55F Duple-bodied Bedford YMT usually used on the 606; and some second-hand stock, including a Leyland Leopard/Marshall ex-Ribble and two Alexander-bodied AEC Swifts, one from Cardiff and the other ex-Grampian.

For many years the *Landside* and inter-terminal

services at London's Heathrow Airport were provided by **Whyte's Coaches** of Colnbrook, who also worked a Rail-Air Link between the Airport and Feltham Station, but this was withdrawn in 1981. The Airport work is now undertaken by Ralph's Coaches Ltd.

When LT withdrew 98B after the overtime strike in January 1966, a number of operators tried their hand at the circuitous route from Rayners Lane Station to Ruislip Station (only three stops apart on the 'tube'), incuding Thamesmead, but in May 1971 B. J. Cheek of Kenton, trading as **Elmtree Coaches** took over. This operator has used a number of second-hand buses on the route but two Bedfords with Willowbrook 002 bodies were purchased during the 1970s. However, during the early part of 1982 vehicles failures led to the company hiring two BL class Bristol LH buses from London Transport to maintain the service.

In November 1977 a service from Patchetts Green to Boreham Wood was started by **Campbell Consultants Ltd**, but by mid-1978 this had ceased. On November 3, 1980 **Franklin's Coaches** of Boreham Wood initiated a peak hours partial replacement of LT 299 between its home town and Potters Bar, and another similar route became HC1, but this succumbed in March 1983. The company still runs a shoppers service between the industrial estate and beautiful downtown Boreham Wood using an ex-Grampian AEC Swift, always immaculately turned out in its two-tone blue livery.

At the north-west corner of LT's area is the Breach Barns mobile home park, where a minibus service is operated by **Godfrey Davis (Parks) Ltd** between the site and the Green Man public house at Waltham Abbey, giving a connection with LT buses. Two Ford Transits are used, and the company hopes to extend the route to the Waltham Abbey shopping area.

At one of LT's extremities, **Wards of Epping** runs a service based on the former London Country route 381. The Wards route retains the same number but cuts back the service from Harlow to run Broadley Common to Coopersale Common via

*Right:* **Elmtree Coaches used for many years this ex-Thames Valley Bristol LS5G on its 98B service between Rayners Lane and Ruislip.**

*Right:* **A number of the Lewingtons Bordabus routes were double-deck, such as the Romford-Waltham Cross service on which this ex-Western SMT Alexander-bodied Daimler Fleetline is seen.**

*Left:* **Continental Pioneer used much ex-London Transport stock on its Richmond Hill service, such as this RF type AEC Regal IV with Metro-Cammell body, numbered 50.**

*Below:* **This Weymann-bodied AEC Reliance was new to Salford Corporation, and passed via Selnec and Colchester Corporation to Lewingtons. It is seen on Bordabus route 6 in December 1981.**

Epping. Latterly, two ex-London Country RP class AEC Reliance/Park Royal DP49F vehicles were used to maintain the service, but in May 1982 operation of the 381 was handed over to **Lee-Roy Coaches** of Kelvedon Hatch. During June 1983 the route was cut back from Toothill to Moreton but at the other end was extended from Epping Green to Roydon.

For many years, **L&A Coaches** of Hornchurch ran a service from Rainham Station to the Murex Factory at Rainham Ferry, and although the primary purpose of this peak hours service was to carry Murex employees nevertheless it was licensed as a stage service. However, in late 1977 this became a Murex contract, later being worked by the Seven Kings Motor Co.

After the prolonged strike of LT platform staff in the summer of 1958, a number of routes was axed once services were restored, and a couple of these were in the Gidea Park/Hornchurch area, the replacements being provided by independents. A network of services was built up by **Super Coaches** of Upminster and its subsidiary, **Upminster & District**, using a variety of ex-LT stock including RTs, in a pleasant blue livery. After Super withdrew, City Coach Lines of Kings Cross had a go, followed by Blue Line, Coppins Coaches and finally some company that sounds like a refugee from a Rogers and Hammerstein musical, called **DoRayMe** (an operator of note?). DoRayMe had a trio of routes radiating from County Park Estate to Gidea Park, Hornchurch and Upminster plus a schools service, the latter being enlarged and extended, in 1981. DoRayMe invariably used an ex-Trent Roe-bodied Atlantean and its ex-Waveney AEC Swift on these services, the buses being garaged on the premises of the well-known contract operator **Lewington Coach Hire Services** of Abridge, this latter firm providing substitute vehicles for DoRayMe in the event of breakdowns, etc, and during 1981 the DoRayMe name ceased to be used, the services being licensed to Lewingtons.

In April 1981 Lewingtons introduced route 6, which was marketed as Bordabus, fringing for most of its journey on either Eastern National or LT borders. The route was from Brentwood Station to Collier Row with garage journeys to Abridge, and it was worked with some ex-East Kent AEC Reliances with Park Royal dual-purpose bodies, painted in a special Bordabus livery. Double-deckers were often used on 6 'shorts' between Abridge and Harold Hill. Flushed with the success of 6 (which caused the withdrawal of Eastern National 263), Lewingtons started many routes with varying degrees of success, or less. On July 25, 1981 route 7 was introduced between Woodhall Parade and Harold Hill but lack of support saw its withdrawal within weeks; it was restarted to a limited timetable on schooldays as from September 8, 1981 but two weeks later was curtailed completely. At the end of October route 8 was introduced three days a week, between Romford and Waltham Cross via Debden and Chigwell Row, whilst 'shoppers special' route 9 plied once-weekly between Waltham Cross and Southend via Chigwell Row and Brentford. November 28, 1981 saw LT return to the Gidea Park area with its Romford to County Park Estate 256, and this had a direct bearing on the withdrawal of the ex-DoRayMe routes 2 and 5. By May 1982 Lewingtons had ceased to trade and the DoRayMe proprietor took over once again, trading as **Bordabus Ltd**, and operating some excursions to Walton-on-Naze (route 14) and Clacton (15) under the Bordacoach name, during the summer of 1982. In September of that year the two remaining Hornchurch area routes were withdrawn, although in October 1982 three new 'shoppers' services were introduced. The 99 was a limited stop service as per 9 to Southend, whilst 14A was as per 14 but cut back to Colchester although extended at the London end from Waltham Cross to Cheshunt, which was also the start for 16, to Maidstone.

Finally, to the centre of London and **Obsolete Fleet**. Apart from sightseeing services worked on behalf of London Transport, on April 1, 1983 the company introduced a number of Saturday and Sunday services to the south coast, using ex-LT DMS Daimler Fleetlines carrying yellow 'express' blinds. Introduced as the 600, Elephant and Castle via Camberwell, Peckham, Bromley and 601 (from the Elephant basically via A23), passengers transferred from the latter to the 600 at a certain point. However, this was not a successful arrangement, and the 601 was withdrawn after a few weeks.

In an article such as this I feel that the municipals would be mentioned, to complete the picture. **Reading Transport** X1 enters the LT area at Slough and works through the heart of it to Aldgate, even using the Minories LT bus station as its City terminus, whilst the other X1, that operated by **Southend Transport** comes into LT-land in the Rainham area and stays therein until its terminus, at Heathrow. **Camden Borough Council** operates a minibus service within the large cemetery at Finchley, being a legacy from when the cemetery was an out-of-town establishment. London Transport also operates its 128 on behalf of **Hillingdon Council**, with Hillingdon legends and livery on the BL class buses.

*Footnote:* Since this article was written, the ex-Orpington & District routes were acquired from Tillingbourne by Metrobus. Around the same time (Autumn 1983) Obsolete Fleet ceased trading. Late in 1983 there was an hiatus in Mole Valley operations which were resumed in modified form.